INTERNET
getting started!

ISBN: 2-7460-1227-8
Original edition: ISBN: 2-7460-1084-4

ENI Publishing LTD

500 Chiswick High Road
London W4 5RG

Tel: 020 8956 2320
Fax: 020 8956 2321

e-mail: publishing@ediENI.com
http://www.eni-publishing.com

WAY IN collection directed by Corinne Hervo

Foreword

This book is aimed at true beginners, who have not get encountered the Internet. It has the answers to all the main questions newcomers have and gives a step-by-step guide to the services available over the Internet.

The first part of the book looks at choosing a connection and a service provider and gives you the information you will need to get connected.

Once you are online you can refer to the second part to find out about surfing the Web and using search engine tools (both directories and indexes).

In the third part you will learn about e-mail, which is one of the most popular Internet services. You will go onto discover newsgroups, online chat and Webcams in part 4.

Part 5 consists of information about downloading files (such as plug-ins, demos and freeware) and file compression tools.

The book ends with some general information about security, the different governing bodies of the Internet and the possibilities for the Internet in the future.

This book is for reading, but also for learning. While you are using your computer, go ahead and try out some of the actions described by following the example. Keep this book close to your computer and you will find it a useful reference for finding a function or term you have forgotten.

You will not just find information about the features covered, but also tips on what not to do, what not to forget as well as handy shortcuts to help you save time.

Throughout this book, you will come across the following symbols:

indicates a comment with extra information about the heading.

indicates a handy tip.

Table of Contents

Table of Contents

Table of Contents

E-mail — 3rd Part

Getting used to your e-mail tools — Chapter 3.1

Dealing with messages — Chapter 3.2

Lists — Chapter 3.3

# of Contents

Internet discussion and chat — 4th Part

Discussion forums — Chapter 4.1

Live chat — Chapter 4.2

Webcams — Chapter 4.3

Table of Contents

Downloads/compression — 5th Part

Download services — Chapter 5.1

Downloading files — Chapter 5.2

Compressed files — Chapter 5.3

Table of Contents

More information — 6th Part

Table of Contents

Appendices

If you are planning to reach the Internet from a Cybercafe or from a computer which is already set up, you can skip to chapter 1.2. Chapter 1.1 deals with how to connect your computer to the Internet.

1st Part

Your Internet connection

Getting onto the Internet

Although the Internet is made up of complicated technologies, there is no need to understand them before you can use it. Below you will find all the information you need to get started.

ACCESSING THE INTERNET

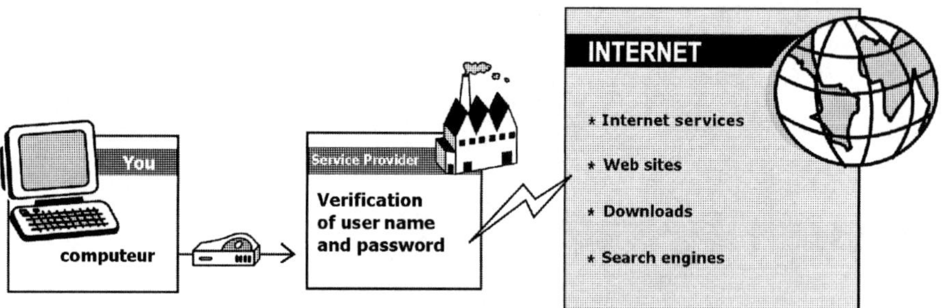

This diagram illustrates the principle of Internet access for home users.

- To access the Internet, you will need a contract with a service provider. You will also need a modem for your computer, which will communicate with the service provider, or, more precisely, with the service provider's computer.
- The service provider's computer will ask for your username, or login, and your password. If these are correct, you will then be able to use the Internet.
- You can see that the key points for connecting are:
  - a connection method and a modem appropriate to this method,
  - a contract with an Internet service provider (ISP),
  - a computer with a modem that has been configured to know which ISP it should contact.
- This is known as a computer with a configured modem and connection.

There are many different methods of connecting to the Internet, ranging from the standard to the most powerful.

CHOOSING A CONNECTION METHOD

- **Using a standard telephone line** (PSTN):

  The modem is plugged into a telephone socket and communicates with the ISP at a maximum of 56 K/sec.
  All the time the modem is connected to the Internet, the telephone line is unavailable. The cost of the calls is charged at local rate.

  Prices vary, but as a guide, you can expect to pay between £40 and £50 for a 56K modem in the UK. If you pay for the time you spend online at the local call rate, five hours will cost around £5.50 (with BT). You may choose an ISP subscription that includes the call charges. If you do, the prices (and inclusive call time) will vary.

- **Using an ISDN line**:

  The modem is still connected to a telephone socket (although it differs slightly from a standard telephone jack), but communicates with the ISP at 64K/sec.
  During the call the telephone line is unavailable, and the call is charged at the local rate.

  Here again, prices differ, but expect to pay an installation fee of £100, and £25 for fifteen hours of Internet access per month (including the call charges, line rental and ISP subscription).

- **Using a cable connection** (through a cable operator):

  This method is only available if you live in an area that has cable access. The main drawback is that you will share the cable capacity with any other users connected at the same time, making it advisable to avoid peak periods.

  This means that the maximum speed of 512K/sec is not guaranteed. You are billed for the subscription (plus modem rental charges - if applicable). Your phone line is not used.

  Typical costs in the UK are £150 for the modem, followed by a monthly fee of £20 (for unmetered access), or a monthly subscription of £30 (which includes modem rental).

- **Using an ADSL line** (only available to PC users for the moment):

  This method uses an existing, un-used bandwidth in your standard telephone line (data bandwidths), without encroaching on the bandwidth used by your telephone.
  To make use of this bandwidth, you need to install a filter to separate voice and data. Your PC will need a specific modem and an Ethernet card.
  With this method, your telephone line is not in use during Internet connections, and connection speeds are much faster (up to 512 K/sec for home users, and 2 M/sec for businesses).
  BT plans to make this service available to 80% of the UK population.

  This option will require an investment of £150 (for the installation), and £40 per month for line rental.

- **Using a satellite link or dedicated line**:

  These are solutions for businesses with significant Internet requirements. They are billed on a monthly basis at between £400 and £800.

For home computers, each different connection solution requires a different sort of modem. It pays to decide on your connection method before investing in a modem.

Once you have decided how you want to connect to the Internet, you will need to choose the ISP who will provide you with the service that suits you best.

CHOOSING A SERVICE PROVIDER

- A good way to begin would be by asking around friends and family, especially those who use the Internet for the same purposes as you want to.

- One of the main criteria is to choose an ISP who bills calls at the local rate. Most ISPs use special local rate numbers. The availability of some services can vary from place to place, so check with people in the neighbourhood for the best offers.

Asking people who have a similar lifestyle and family to yours (teenaged children, for instance) can give you a good idea of how much to budget for Internet use and how much time you can expect to spend connected to the Internet.

- If you choose the cable or ADSL options, charges vary little between providers. However, there are two main differences between PSTN providers:

Providers who charge	were the first on the market. Nearly all of them now offer subscriptions that include an allowance of pre-paid call time.
Free providers	are also starting to propose call-inclusive offers, the difference being that they do not charge a subscription fee to access their services.

- Free ISPs are becoming more and more popular and offer a similar level of service to ISPs who charge a subscription fee. Many of these providers were created by commercial groups who wanted to be sure that future Internet-consumers would have a good quality access.
- An important point to bear in mind is the price and quality of the **helpline** (or helpdesk).

  This is the service you will call if you need help as you discover the Internet. You may find that you call often to begin with and could be on the phone for a long time. You should make sure that the helpline is available when you think you might need it and that the call charges are not too high. Current call charges can be anything from local rate to 50p/minute.
- Of course, you can always try out several ISPs before you make your final choice, but it is a good idea not to give your e-mail address to too many people before you have fixed on a permanent one (see also Part 3 - E-mail).
- AOL is a provider (who charges) who stands out from the others by offering guided Internet access, which is particularly suitable for beginners. Some find this reassuring, others feel too smothered.

The browser and e-mail program provided by AOL are specific to the provider, so if you decide to leave AOL, you will have to learn how to use new software.

AOL presents itself as an "online service provider" rather than an ISP, because the user is given guided access to the Internet. The browser tools are accompanied by explanations and short tutorials. The helpline is charged at local rate.

Having looked at all the different connection options and chosen your ISP, you are now ready to install everything necessary to connect.

THE DIFFERENT STEPS TO CONNECTION

1 - Installing your modem

- If the modem is not already installed, you will need to do this. Refer to the instructions for physically installing the modem, then for installing the necessary driver (a file that will enable the modem to communicate with your computer's operating system).
- Before you start to install your connection, it is a good idea to check that your modem is correctly installed:

On a PC:

- Right-click the **My Computer** icon on the desktop.
- Choose the **Properties** option.
- Click the **Device Manager** tab.
- If you can see the modem in the list and its name is correct, then the installation is correct.

On a Mac:

- From the **PPP** menu on the worktop, choose the **Modem** submenu.
- Make sure that the configuration shown corresponds to that of your modem, then close the window.

- If there is a problem, refer to the manual you received with the modem for the correct configuration, or contact the hardware supplier. Your ISP helpline will probably be able to resolve minor problems.

2 - Contacting your chosen ISP

- First, contact the ISP in order to subscribe to the service.
- You will then receive notification from the provider, including information you will need in order to connect to the Internet:
  - your username or login,
  - your password,
  - your e-mail address.

  There will also be more technical information such as:
  - the name of the POP server,
  - the name of the SMTP server,
  - the name of the news server,
  - the telephone number for the ISP's server.
- You should also receive a connection kit (a CD-ROM), which contains a program that will install your connection and the necessary software automatically.

Some connection kits allow you to subscribe to an ISP, without having first contacted the provider.

3 - Installing the connection kit

- The CD-ROM should run automatically, but if it does not, follow the instructions given.
- The program provided by your ISP will carry out the installation of a number of applications automatically:
  - a browser (Internet Explorer or Netscape Navigator),
  - an e-mail and news program (such as Outlook Express or Netscape Messenger).

If any of these applications is already present on your computer, you can still install the ISP's programs. If the version you have is older than that of the ISP, it will be updated and if you have the same version, the ISP's application will replace it.

- The program will then configure these applications (by defining settings such as the names of the POP and SMTP servers) and will then configure your Internet connection. You will need to give some information, such as:
  - your username,
  - your password,
  - your e-mail address.
- If you have chosen AOL as your ISP, the applications provided are specific to AOL. If you have any questions, you will need to call the AOL helpline.
- Once the installation is complete, you will find that the menus contain options (which might be terms like **dial-up networking** and **e-mail** or might be in the name of your ISP) that allow you to access the principle Internet services, such as access to the Web, or to your e-mail. You may also notice that shortcuts have appeared on the desktop. To use these Internet services, either start your browser or e-mail program or choose the menu options (in which case your browser or e-mail program will run automatically).

If you are only using one ISP, your computer will connect to this provider automatically when you launch your browser. However, you can choose to install several connections if you want to use more than one ISP to access the Internet.

Some of the information you receive from your ISP will need to be kept if you want to make use of some of the services available from the Internet. If this information is not communicated when you take out your subscription, contact your ISP to obtain it, then keep it carefully.

KEEPING IMPORTANT TECHNICAL INFORMATION

- **For connecting and surfing**:
  - your username or login for Internet access,
  - your Internet access password,
  - the name of the server and proxy port,
  - your IP address allocation (this is only applicable to users who have a permanent connection, such as ADSL or cable subscribers).
- **For e-mail**:
  - your personal e-mail address,
  - the incoming mail server's address (pop or imap),
  - the outgoing mail server's address (smtp),
  - your username for your inbox,
  - your password for your inbox.

  For an explanation of these terms, refer to Part 3, which deals with e-mail.
- **For discussion groups**:
  - the news or discussion groups server.

These settings will have been added to your browser and e-mail program automatically when you installed the connection kit. You can find them using the following commands:
- in Netscape use **Edit** - **Preferences**
- in Internet Explorer use **Tools** - **Internet Options** - **Connections** tab
- in Outlook Express use **Tools** - **Accounts.**

What can you do on the Internet?

Internet, the Web, e-mail, discussion groups... what does it all mean?

UNDERSTANDING THE DIFFERENT USES OF THE INTERNET

- The term Internet simply describes the network (the wires, basically) that enables you to access the services.
- The most frequently used services are:
  - e-mail,
  - searches for information,
  - file transfers (downloading software, images, videos, music and so on),
  - themed discussion groups.
- Other services include online chat, telephony and webcams.

These services all use the Internet network, but are independent of each other. They are each accessible via a specific protocol and a specific application.

Each Internet service carries a bundle of associated terms. These terms are getting better known as the Internet develops and the number of users increases.

WORDS YOU WILL ALREADY HAVE HEARD

- The table below should give you a better idea of the meanings of these new terms:

service	associated keywords	essential software	where in this book
information search	Websites and Web pages site addresses: http://www.editions-eni.com search engines, browser http://, HTML	**Browsers**: Netscape Navigator (included in the Netscape Communicator suite) Internet Explorer, Opera	Part 2

service	associated keywords	essential software	where in this book
electronic mail	e-mail, mail mailbox, e-mail addresses: publishing@edi-ENI.com the "@" sign (at)	**E-mail programs** Netscape Messenger (included in the Netscape Communicator suite) Outlook Express (included with Internet Explorer) Eudora Light etc...	Part 3
discussion forums	forums newsgroups, news usenet, communities discussion group address: uk.rec.gardening, chat, IRC, channels, messenger, ICQ, video-conferencing, webcam	These services are very different from one another and use different tools	Part 4
file transfer	download, compressed files Zip zipped MP3 music, software updates	Generally, your browser is all you should need to download files	Part 5

What can you do on the Internet?

All these terms are listed in the glossary at the end of this book.

Now you are ready to surf, ready to discover a universe of text, pictures, movies, sounds, special effects... This section will give you all the information you need to avoid getting lost in "Cyberspace".

2nd Part

The Web

Working with a browser

Along with e-mail, the Web is the most popular service available through the Internet, so much so that the two terms are commonly confused. However, the Web is in fact only a part of the Internet. It is accessed via a browser.

UNDERSTANDING THE WEB AND THE ROLE OF BROWSERS

- The Web, or World Wide Web, is a collection of over a billion pages that contain mostly text, images, graphs and photos. It is growing all the time.
- Your browser lets you see the content of these pages. When you installed your Internet connection, your browser was configured either automatically or manually.
- The most popular browsers are Internet Explorer and Netscape Navigator. The former is installed automatically on your PC with Windows 98 (or Windows Me); it is also installed on the Mac. The latter is included in the Netscape Communicator suite. Both are freely available to download from Microsoft's site (http://www.microsoft.com) or Netscape's site (http://www.netscape.com).

To access a Web site you will first need to start your browser so that it appears on the screen.

STARTING YOUR BROWSER

On a PC

- Click the **Start** button on the taskbar (at the bottom of the Windows desktop) and drag the mouse pointer to the **Programs** option.
- Depending on the browser:
  - click the **Internet Explorer** option,
  - or point to the **Netscape Communicator** option then click **Netscape Navigator**.

On a Mac

- Click the [Apple] menu in the menu bar at the top of the screen and drag the mouse pointer to the **Applications** option.
- Depending on the browser:
  - click the **Microsoft Internet Explorer** option,
  - or click the **Netscape Navigator** option or **Netscape Communicator**.

There may be a shortcut (the term for PC users) or alias (the term for Mac users) on your desktop that represents one or the other of these browsers. If this is the case, double-click this icon to launch the browser.

The application (your browser software) appears in a window. If you are not already connected to the Internet, the dial-up connection process will start automatically. Let the modem call your ISP, who will verify your username and password.

THE BASIC TOOLS IN YOUR BROWSER

The Microsoft Internet Explorer window.

Working with a browser

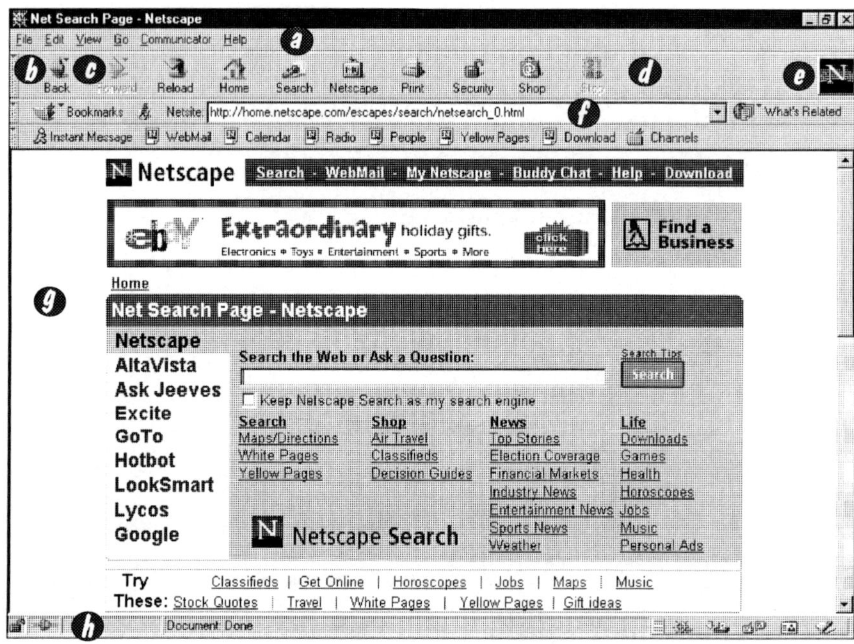

The Netscape Navigator window.

It is possible that what you see on your screen does not correspond exactly to what is shown in these illustrations. However, it is nevertheless important to pick out the basic tools in your browser.

a. The menu bar.

b. The **Back** button.

c. The **Forward** button.

d. The **Stop** button.

e. This icon might be Netscape's, Internet Explorer's, or your ISP's.

f. The address bar.

g. The Web page display.

h. The status or progression bar.

Below you can learn how to use these essential tools. They were created in Illinois in 1993 by the creators of Mosaic, the first browser, and are so efficient that all current browsers use them. This means that, if you change from one browser to another, you will never be completely lost.

DISPLAYING YOUR FIRST WEB PAGE

- Click in the text box on the address bar (f).
- Delete the text that is there and replace it with the address of the site you want to visit. For example, type **http://www.editions-eni.com**.
- Confirm by pressing ↵.
- When you type a Web address, remember:
  - do not use apostrophes,
  - do not use spaces,
  - the only characters allowed (apart from letters and numbers) are the forward slash (/), hyphens (-), underscores (_) and full stops (.).
- The (e) icon begins to turn and the status bar (h) indicates how close the page is to loading.
- When the former stops turning and the latter reads **Done** or **Document: Done**, the page you wanted is fully displayed in the window (g) (if you typed the address of a site, the site's homepage is shown).

If you cannot see all of the page contents, use the scroll bars to the right and at the bottom of the window to discover the entire page.
If the page takes too long to display and you lose patience, click the **Stop** button (d) to stop the page from loading, then try another address.

Working with a browser

The Web uses a hyperlink system, in which you go from one page to another by clicking on hyperlinks. In each page you will find one or more links. When a link is activated, it starts another page loading, in which you will find yet more hyperlinks.

ACTIVATING HYPERLINKS IN A PAGE

- To find the where the links are in page, move the mouse pointer around. When the pointer takes the shape of a hand, there is a link.

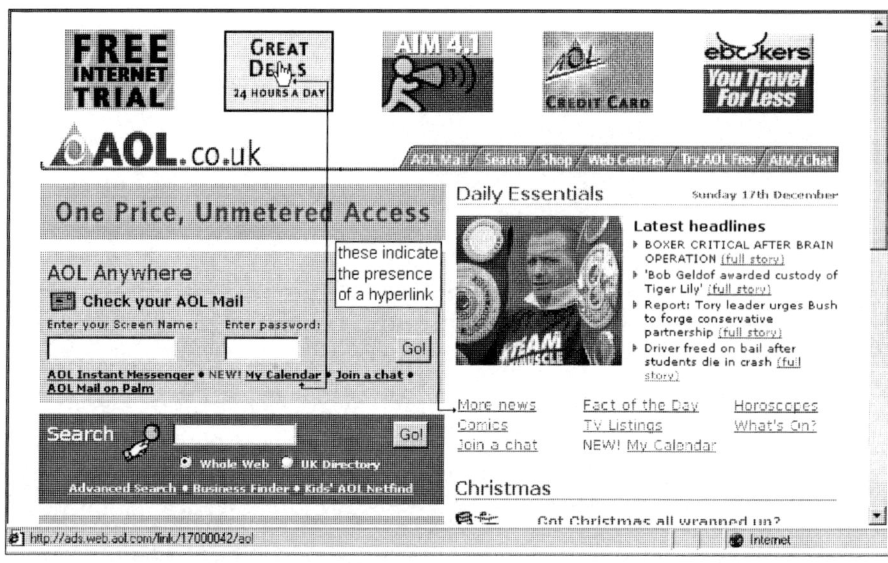

A link might take the form of certain words in the text or an image.

When you point to a link, the address of the page to which it leads appears on the status bar at the bottom of the window.

- Traditionally, text that is associated with a link appears in blue and is underlined, but this norm is less and less applied to Web pages as designers place more importance on the aspect of pages. The best way to find links is to move the mouse pointer all around the page, not forgetting to use the scroll bars, of course!
- To activate a link and display a new page, click the link in question.

- Some links allow you to go from page to page within the same site, in which case the beginning of the address (the site or server's address) stays the same:

- Other links will send you to a different site and you will notice a change in the appearance of the pages and a different address in the browser's address bar (f).

  Happy surfing!

If you have followed a few links as you have been surfing, you may decide you want to go back to a previous page, perhaps in order to see some of the other links.

RETURNING TO A PREVIOUS PAGE

- As you surf by clicking hyperlinks, Web browsers keep track of all the pages you pass through. They keep a list of the address of every page you have visited. This list, called the **History**, allows you to retrace your steps.
- Click the **Previous** (b) button.

  The browser displays the last page you viewed.

- To see all the pages you have visited, keep clicking the button.
- The **Forward** (c) button becomes available as soon as you click the **Back** button. Use this button to move forward through the sites you have already visited.

Working with a browser

If you have visited several pages and clicking the **Back** button does not retrace your steps, there is a possibility that one of the links you have clicked has opened a new page in a new window of the browser. In this case, the browser "forgets" the pages you have visited in another window, but you can still find previous pages by clicking in the different browser windows that are open on the desktop.

*The **Back** and **Forward** buttons described above allow you to find pages that you have visited during the current session. However, if you close the browser, you will not be able to go back to these pages. As you surf, you will certainly come across interesting pages which you want to re-visit. Saving an address can be compared to marking the page of a book, as you can then find the page again quickly. Netscape calls these markers **Bookmarks** and Internet Explorer uses the term **Favorites**.*

SAVING THE ADDRESS OF AN INTERESTING PAGE

With Netscape Navigator

- To create a bookmark, display the page you want to bookmark and, in the menu bar (a), choose **Communicator - Bookmarks - Add Bookmark** or Ctrl **D**.
- To go to a bookmark quickly, choose **Communicator - Bookmarks** on the menu bar, then:

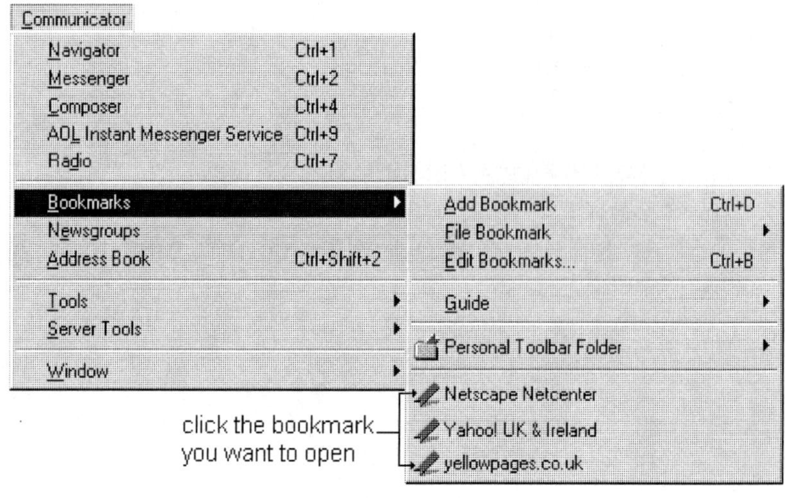

The Web

With Internet Explorer

- To create a favourite, display the page you want as a favourite and choose **Favorites - Add to Favorites** from the menu bar.

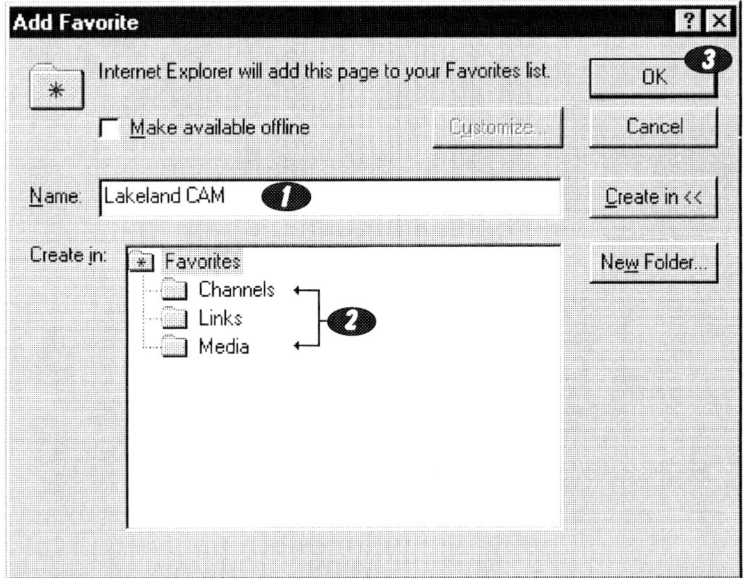

1. Change the name of the page if the one shown is not suitable.
2. If you like, select the folder in which you want to save the favourite.
3. Create the favourite.

- You can find your favourites by clicking **Favorites** on the menu bar, then clicking the name of the favourite you want to display.

Your favourites or bookmarks are created on the hard drive of your computer, which means that if you access the Web using another computer, you will not be able to use your bookmarks or favourites. Netscape Navigator and Internet Explorer have different page-marking systems and they are mutually incompatible: you will not be able to recuperate bookmarks from Netscape Navigator to use them as Internet Explorer favourites or vice versa.

Working with a browser

Information from the Internet that you can see on your screen can be saved on your hard drive so that you can use it again later. Doing this will also help you to understand what happens in your computer when you consult Web pages.

KEEPING A TEXT ONLY COPY

While you are surfing the Web, you never actually go "into" a server, but simply "repatriate" files onto your computer. Everything that appears on your screen is actually on your hard drive during the time you are connected:

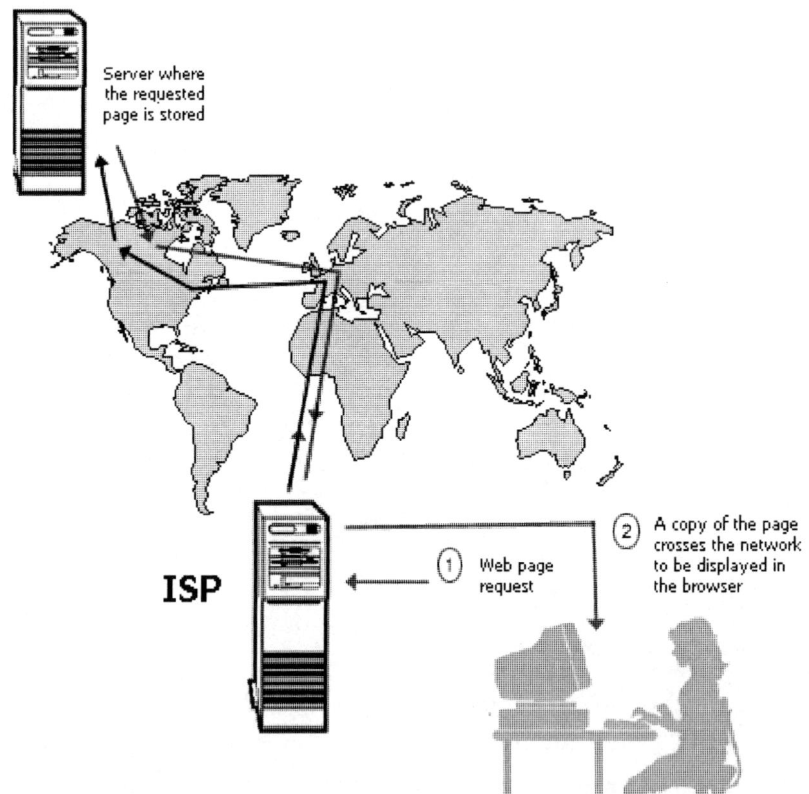

This means that you can save this information on your hard drive.

First method

With this method, you use the Web page to create a new document on your computer. You will be able to display this document later in your browser without being connected to the Internet.

- Display the Web page in question in your browser.
- In the menu bar (a), choose **File - Save As**.

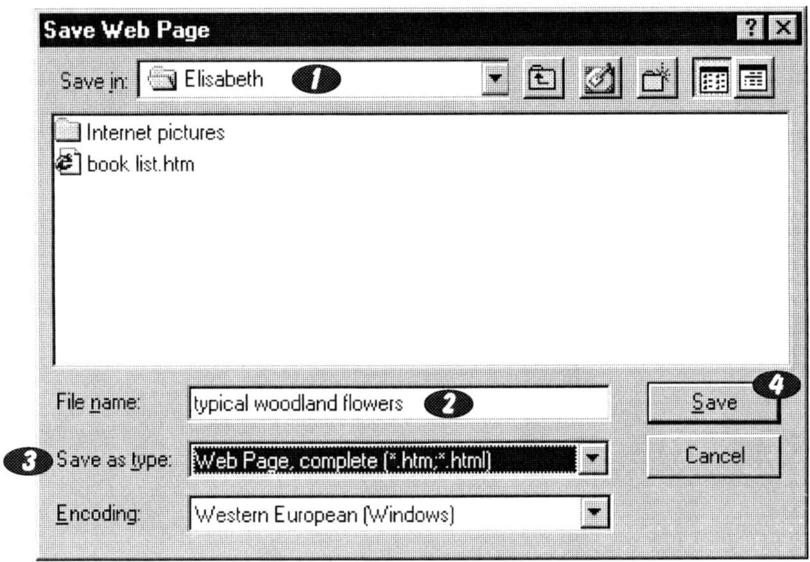

1. Choose the folder on your hard drive in which you want to save the page.
2. Give the document a name.
3. In Internet Explorer, choose the type of file you want to save:

Web Page, complete	to save all the information in the page, including the frames, images, and style sheets.
Web Archive, single file	if you want to save all the information in the page in one file in MHT format.
Web Page, HTML only	to save the current page without any images, sounds, or other associated files.
Text File	if you only want to save the text of the current page.

4. Save the page.

In most browsers you cannot save images contained in a Web page by using the File - Save As command, but only the text. The exception is Internet Explorer 5 (or later).

Second method

When you choose this method, you actually copy all or some of the text contained in the Web page, then place it in an open document in another application, such as Word, WordPad, Simple Text or PowerPoint.

- Open the Web page in question in the browser.
- If you want to copy all the text in the page, choose **Edit - Select All** from the menu bar (a).
  If you are only interested by part of the text, drag to select this text, being careful to select up to the last word.
- Choose **Edit - Copy** on the menu bar (a).
- Go to the document into which you want to place the text (in another application).
- In the other application, use the **Edit - Paste** command.

You will notice that a number of Web pages have a dark coloured background with light or white coloured text.
When you copy text like this using the second method, you will not be able to see anything on the page when you paste the text into a new document! This is because you have copied white (or light coloured) text onto a white background. Solve the problem by selecting the text and choosing a darker colour.

Web pages very often include pictures (drawings or photographs) that you can also copy onto your hard drive, using the method below.

KEEPING A COPY OF A PICTURE FROM A WEB PAGE

- Open the Web page in question in the browser.
- Point the mouse pointer at the picture.
- Right-click the picture (or, for Mac users, hold the Ctrl key down as you click the mouse button).
- In the menu that appears, choose the **Save Picture As** option.
- Choose the folder in which you want to save the picture and give it a name.

Be careful: some pictures and texts are protected by copyright. If they are, you cannot use them as if they belonged to you and especially not for commercial purposes.

You may find that it gets tiring to read pages on the screen all the time and want to print them. Printing can also be useful to keep a record of an online purchase, or if you want to send a form by the post.

PRINTING A WEB PAGE

- First make sure that your printer is ready for use (that it is plugged in, switched on, has enough paper and so on).
- Display the Web page you want in the browser.
- Choose **File - Print** from the menu bar (a).
- In the printing dialog box, choose the options you want and then enter to print the page.

Working with a browser

Using Internet Explorer

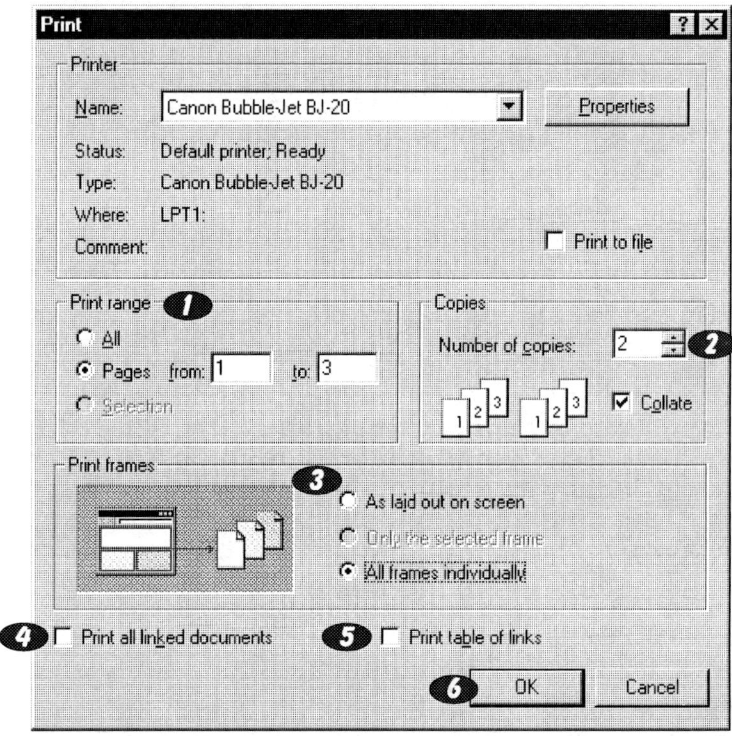

1. Choose whether you want to print **All** the pages, a selection of **Pages**, or the current **Selection**.
2. Indicate the number of copies you want.
3. If necessary, decide how you want to print the frames in the page (see below):

As laid out on screen	will print all the frames as they appear on the screen.
Only the selected frame	to print only the active frame, which is the last one in which you clicked before choosing to print (watch out, you could get a surprise here).

All frames individually will print each of the frames one after the other.

4. Do you want to print all documents that are linked to the active page?

5. Do you want to print a list of all the links in the page?

6. Start printing.

The **Print frames** section is worth a closer look. Some Web pages, like the one shown below, are made up of several frames:

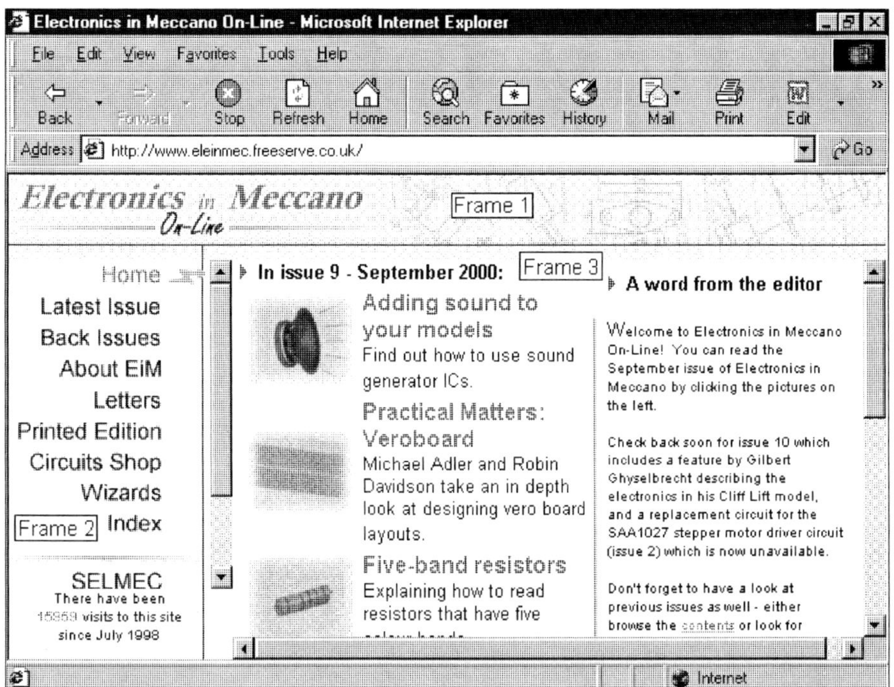

Frame 1 remains static at the top of the page. You can scroll down frames 2 and 3 by using the scroll bars to the right of the frames.

Working with a browser

Technically, the page corresponding to the address that you can see in the address bar is actually a group of different pages, each with its own distinct address, which you cannot see. The printing options allow you to chose which frame(s) you want to print.

Using Netscape Navigator

The printing dialog box in this browser contains fewer options:

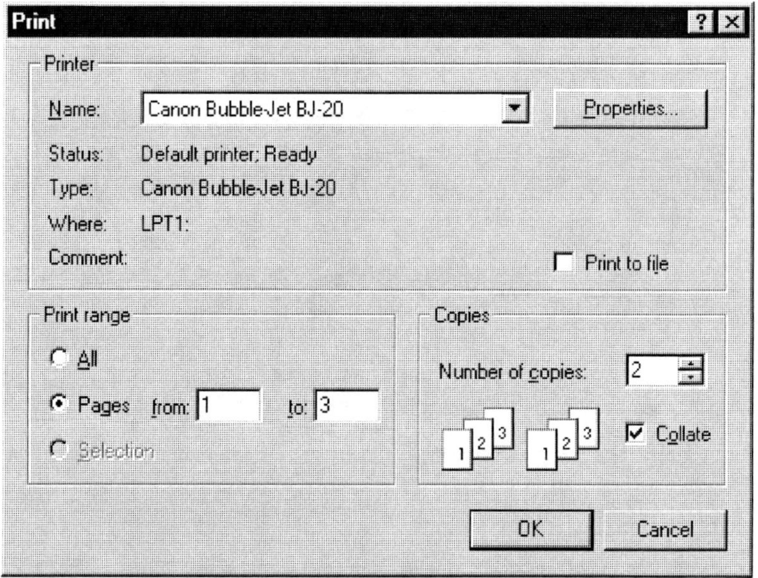

You cannot choose to print several frames, nor the documents linked to the active page, nor the list of links in the page. To print a frame, you need to click in the frame before activating the print command.

However, Netscape Navigator does have a preview function that lets you see exactly what you are about to print.

- Display the preview window by activating **File - Print Preview**.

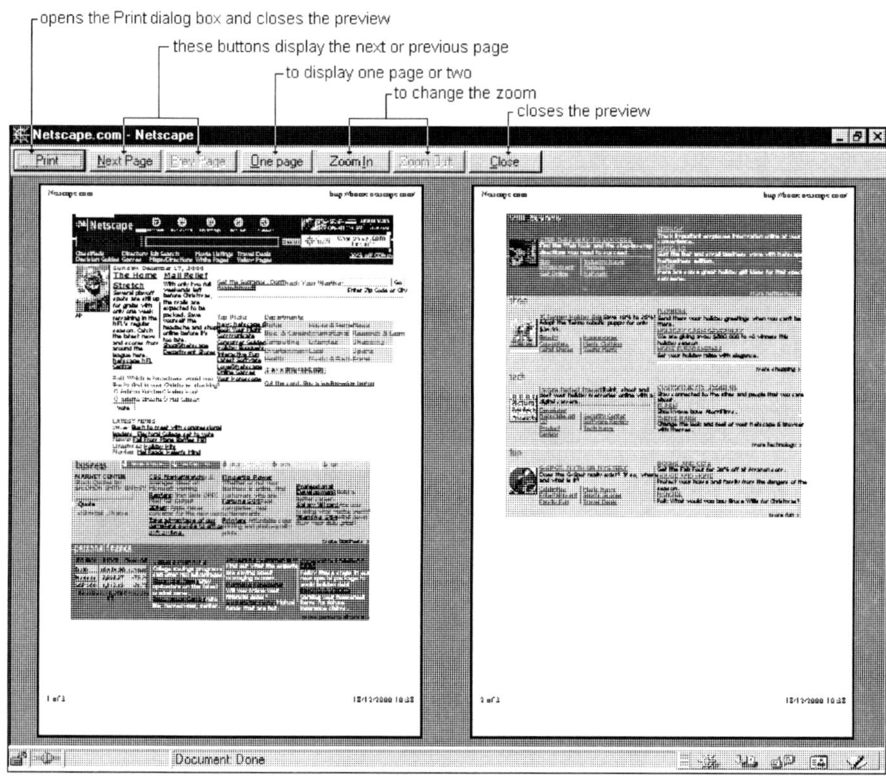

This window lets you know how many pages will be printed and shows you what will appear on those pages (which helps you to avoid unpleasant surprises when you are printing pages that include frames).

Finding things on the Web

The Web is vast, made up of more than one billion pages. To find those pages you want to see, search tools are indispensable.

CHOOSING YOUR SEARCH TOOL

- Two different types of search tool exist for the Web. You will need to know which is which in order to make the best use of them:
  - directories, listing pages grouped by theme,
  - search engines.
- Directories are the best option if you want to search according to a general theme such as "street theatre", or if you want to find the site of, for example, an Irish whiskey distiller.

  In the following pages, the example used is the UK and Ireland version of the Yahoo! directory (www.yahoo.co.uk). Of course, there are other directory services that work in the same way as Yahoo!, some of which are listed at the end of this book.

- Index-based search engines work by selecting pages that contain specified keywords. For this reason, they are better adapted to searching for a precise subject, or for pictures, sounds or technical aspects of the page.

  Later in this chapter, you can see the example of the Google search engine (www.google.com).

Web search tools are sites just like the others. You can access them by typing their address, no matter who your ISP is and their services are free.

Why not start by looking at theme-based directories, taking Yahoo!'s UK site as an example.

DISCOVERING DIRECTORIES

- The creators of directories define categories, or themes, which are then divided into sub-categories; themselves further divided into more sub-categories.

- The sites that are listed in a directory are classed in one or more of these categories. When the number of sites in one category becomes too high, the directory's technicians will create subdivisions to clarify the category.
- To discover the way in which Yahoo! categories work, open your browser and type the site's address: **http://www.yahoo.co.uk**.

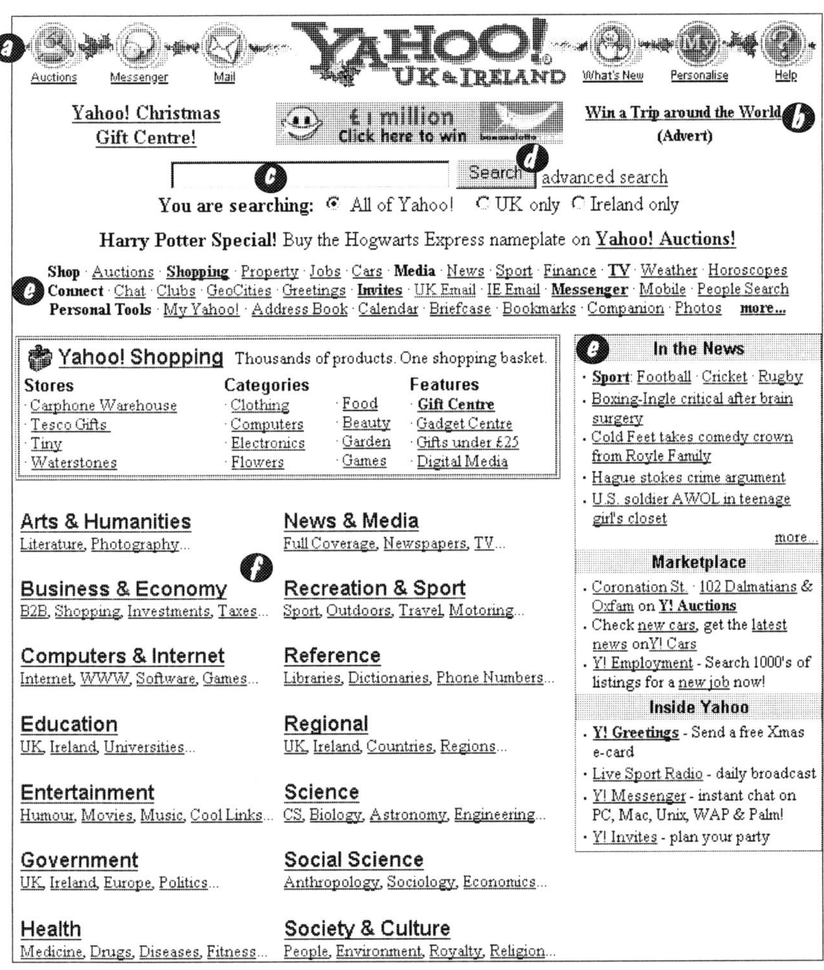

The homepage that you can see on your screen may differ slightly from this illustration.

Finding things on the Web

a. This is the Yahoo.co.uk homepage header.

b. A scrolling advertisement (these sorts of advertisements provide the site's income).

c. Text box in which you can type keywords.

d. The **Search** button you click to start a search for the keywords.

e. Various Yahoo! services (which aim to encourage you to surf the site and therefore generate publicity).

f. Yahoo! categories (see below).

- Click, for example, on the **Science** category, which is one of the main Yahoo! categories.
- Now you can see a list of the sub-categories in **Science**:

- Acoustics *(60)*
- Agriculture *(2028)* NEW!
- Alternative *(1061)*
- Amateur Science *(19)*
- Animals, Insects, and Pets@
- Anthropology and Archaeology@
- Artificial Life *(132)* NEW!
- Ask an Expert *(21)*
- Astronomy *(2541)* NEW!
- Aviation and Aeronautics *(238)*
- Bibliographies *(6)*
- Biology *(16544)* NEW!
- Booksellers@
- Chats and Forums *(45)*
- Chemistry *(1281)*
- Cognitive Science *(95)*
- Complex Systems *(23)*
- Computer Science *(1578)*
- Dictionaries *(28)*
- Earth Sciences *(2725)* NEW!
- Ecology *(752)* NEW!
- Education *(483)* NEW!
- Employment *(47)*
- Energy *(564)*
- Engineering *(4780)* NEW!
- Events *(37)*
- Forensics *(60)*
- Geography *(3088)*
- Geology and Geophysics@
- History *(91)*
- Humour@
- Hydrology@
- Information Technology *(72)*
- Institutes *(62)*
- Journals *(32)*
- Libraries *(34)*
- Life Sciences *(19)*
- Mathematics *(1915)*
- Measurements and Units *(224)*
- Medicine@
- Meteorology@
- Museums and Exhibits *(148)*
- Nanotechnology *(46)*
- News and Media *(143)*
- Oceanography@
- Organisations *(164)*
- Palaeontology@
- People *(41)*
- Physics *(1689)*
- Psychology@
- Religion and Science@
- Research *(166)*
- Science and Technology Policy *(73)*
- Space *(1277)* NEW!
- Sport@
- Web Directories *(44)*

The numbers shown between brackets indicate the number of site addresses available in the subcategory.
The @ character indicates that the subcategory contains further subcategories.

- Click **Life Sciences** (there are 19 addresses available in this subcategory).

a. This is to show where the category is situated: **Science > Life Sciences**.

b. This is the search banner, available in all pages of all the subcategories (see also Making a simple search with Yahoo!).

c. The five subcategories in **Science > Life Sciences**, four of which contain subcategories themselves, indicated by the @ character. The number of sites that the other subcategory contains is shown in brackets.

d. The two sites that are listed in the **Science > Life Sciences** subcategory, which you can visit by clicking the blue underlined text (the hyperlinks).

Finding things on the Web

Now that you have been introduced to the hierarchical structure typical to most directories, you can make your first keyword search.

MAKING A SIMPLE SEARCH WITH YAHOO!

- Go to a page that contains a search banner (a text box accompanied by the **Search** button).
- In the text box, type a keyword that corresponds to the subject which interests you. For example, you could type **architecture**.
- Click the **Search** button.

Yahoo! carries out the search, then presents a page with the results. The top of this page is shown below:

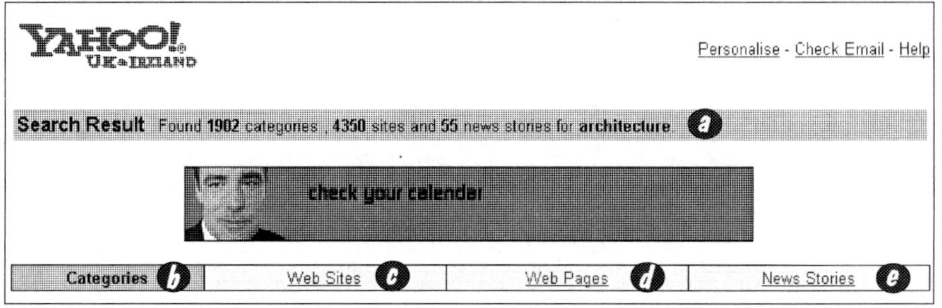

a. Here is a general resume of the search results (in this case, 1902 categories, 4350 sites, and 55 news stories).

b. This choice is not available (you cannot click it with the mouse) because it corresponds to the active page, i.e. the categories listed below the banner.

c. Click here to see a list of the 4350 sites.

d. Click here to see a list of other Web pages where your keyword appears.

e. Click here to see the corresponding news stories.

The four groups of results (categories, Web sites, Web pages and news stories) are always given in the same order.

Here are the first few lines from the categories list. Yahoo! offers a list of all the categories that correspond to your keyword, which appears in bold.

Yahoo! Category Matches (1 - 20 of 1902)

Arts > Design Arts

- **Architecture**

Regional > Countries > United Kingdom > Arts and Humanities > Design Arts

- **Architecture**

Regional > Countries > United Kingdom > England > Counties and Regions > Greater London > Entertainment and Arts

- **Architecture** a

Business and Economy > Business to Business

- **Architecture** 

Regional > Countries > Ireland > Arts and Humanities > Design Arts

- **Architecture**

Arts > Design Arts

- Landscape **Architecture**

Regional > U.S. States > Washington, D.C. > Entertainment and Arts

- **Architecture**

Regional > Countries > United Kingdom > Business and Economy > Business to Business

- **Architecture**

Regional > U.S. States > New York > Cities > New York > Entertainment and Arts

- **Architecture**

Business and Economy > Business to Business > **Architecture**

- Landscape **Architecture** 

Science > Computer Science

- **Architecture**

*You can see where **Architecture** is situated in the hierarchy of categories.*

a. If you click here, you will go to a list of architecture-related sites that are based in the Greater London area.

b. By clicking here, you can see a list of architecture services for businesses.

c. Click this link to see a list of landscape architecture companies.

You will have noticed that this technique lets you move around the Yahoo! categories more rapidly than the "hierarchical" method previously shown.

Below you can see the first few lines from the list of Web sites. Each site is shown with the title of the category in which you can find it:

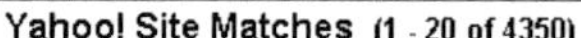

Yahoo! Site Matches (1 - 20 of 4350)

Regional > Countries > United Kingdom > England > Counties and Regions > Greater London >  Entertainment and Arts > **Architecture**

(a) • Architecture Link - for all those interested in **architecture** and design. Includes details on events, latest news, and visits. (b)
- Square-International **Architecture** Workshop - re-scheduled to Spring '98.

Regional > Countries > United Kingdom > England > Counties and Regions > Greater Manchester > Cities and Towns > Manchester > Education > College and University > Manchester Metropolitan University

- Manchester School of **Architecture** - information on courses, studios, and resources.

Regional > Countries > Ireland > Arts and Humanities > Design Arts > **Architecture**

- Archeire - Irish **Architecture** Online - a growing collection of diverse architectural sites intended to heighten awareness of **architecture** within Ireland and to foster international awareness.

Regional > Countries > United Kingdom > Scotland > Counties and Regions > Strathclyde > Cities and Towns > Glasgow > Entertainment and Arts > **Architecture**

- Glasgow Festival of **Architecture** and Design - official web site for the 1999 Festival, designed by Glasgow University and Glasgow School of Art.

Note that the site titles are shown in blue and underlined (this is because they are hyperlinks on which you can click to go to the site) and that they are followed by a short text. Your keyword (in bold type) will appear at least once in the title or the descriptive text.

a. The title of the site called Architecture Link. If you click here, you will go to the site's homepage.

b. A brief description of the site's contents.

c. The Yahoo! category in which the site is listed.

All the sites in the directory have been visited by Yahoo!, and the description has been checked to make sure that it does correspond to the site content. Yahoo! reserves the right to choose not to list sites it visits.

Here are the first results from the **Web Pages** list:

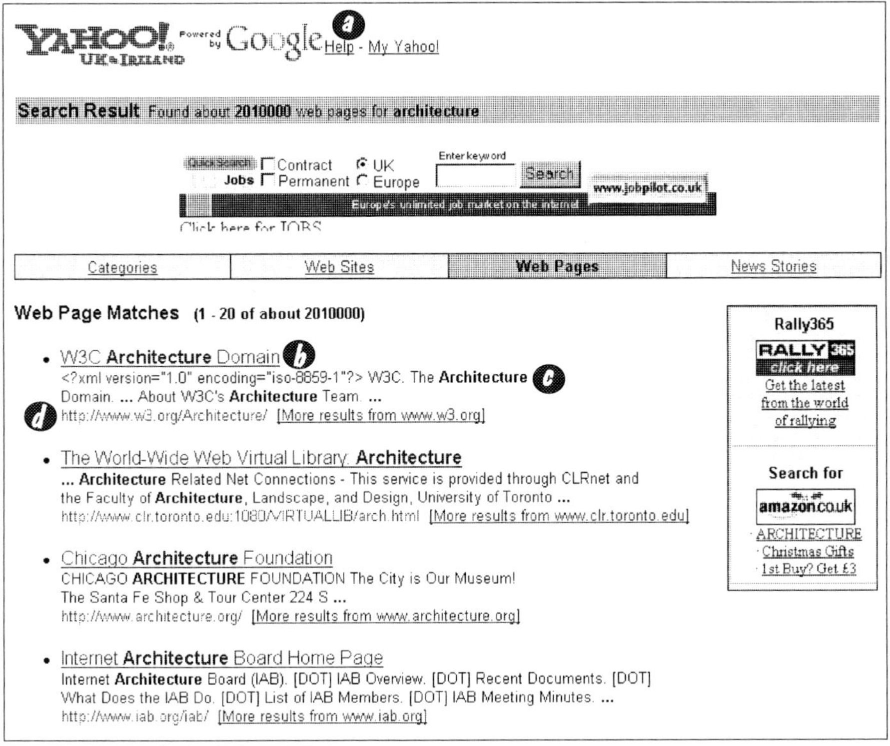

a. Google is a search engine (which you will discover shortly) that works with Yahoo! to complete the results pages. If your keyword does not correspond to any of Yahoo!'s categories, or any of the sites it lists, Google should still be able to provide a list of all the individual pages in which your keyword appears.

b. The title of the page. Click here to go to the page.

c. A few phrases, taken automatically from the text at the top of the page. These phrases often do not make much sense.

d. The address of the site to which the page belongs.

Finding things on the Web

Finally, below are the first results from the news stories that contain your keyword. Yahoo! receives these stories from the main news agencies (such as Reuters and Associated Press):

A directory cannot give you an exhaustive list, but does guarantee a certain quality and classifies results in a way that will help you to find the information you want more quickly. Each site in a directory, no matter how big or small, is described by only a few words. When you use a tool like this to carry out a search, you will only get a result if your keyword appears in the title and/or description that has been accepted by the directory.

A good way to learn more about using directories is to consult their help pages. Yahoo! is also available in several countries, so linguistically-gifted users can increase their searching powers. You will also find a short list of directory services at the end of this book. You may find that the best results come from learning to master one particular directory, rather than switching from one to the other.

If you cannot find what you want by using a directory, you can always try a search engine. You will make better use of this tool if you understand how it works.

DISCOVERING SEARCH ENGINES

- Search engines are index-based tools that reference the **entire contents of all the pages** of the sites they list.
- Basically, each time a search engine lists a new site, a program called a robot is run automatically to analyse all the pages in the site and extract all the words.

  These words are then placed in an index.
- As Web sites and pages change constantly, the robot returns to analyse the pages on a regular basis, thus ensuring that the index is kept up-to-date.
- When you type a keyword to into a search engine, you will be presented with a list of all the pages that contain your keyword.

Finding things on the Web

Remember that a directory proposes a list of sites and takes you to the home page of the site you choose. When using a search engine, you can be directed to any page in the site. The page appears completely out of context and may have nothing to do with what you are actually looking for.

In this example you can see how to use the Google search engine. Google also provides a directory service.

DISCOVERING THE GOOGLE HOMEPAGE

a. A text box for keywords.

b. Click here to refine your search (see REFINING YOUR GOOGLE SEARCH).

c. This is a link to the Google directory (similar to Yahoo!).

Now take a look at how Google works by doing a simple search.

MAKING A SIMPLE SEARCH WITH GOOGLE

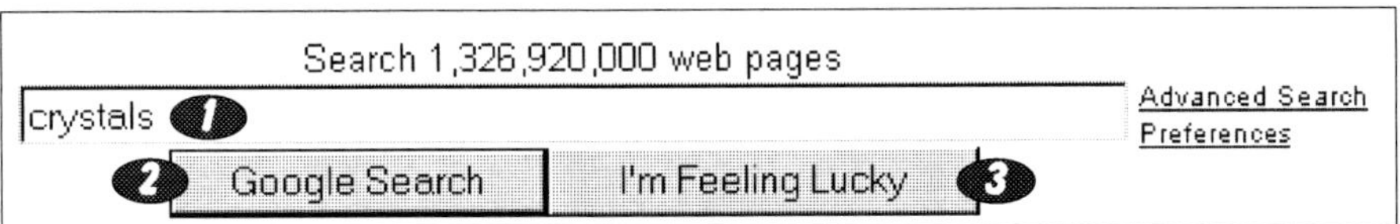

1. Type the keyword you want to find. Here the example uses **crystals**.
2. Click **Google Search** to start searching.
3. If you want to take a gamble, click this button to go straight to the first page from the results.

At the top of the results page, you can see the categories that include your keyword (from the Google Web Directory). Underneath are the pages containing the keyword (from the Google search engine).

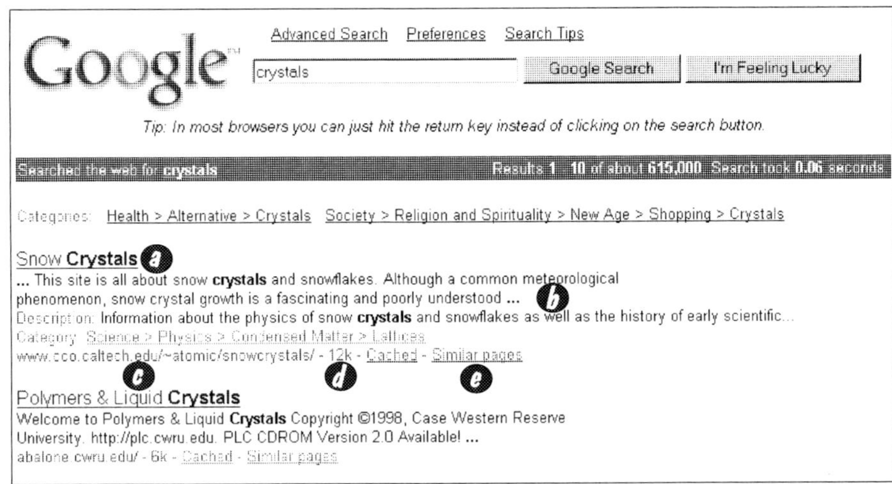

"Crystals" being a fairly general term, Google has found several results:

- **the Web Directory suggests two categories,**
- **the search engine has found around 615 000 pages.**

Finding things on the Web

a. The **page title**: if you click this link, the page will appear in the same window, replacing the list (in which case you will have to use the **Back** button to return to the list).

b. The **first words** in the page, which might give an indication of the page contents.

c. The **page's address**: look at the first part (the domain name) to get an idea of who has created the page (such as a university, a company, or if they are personal pages).

d. The **size of the page**: pages over 60 K are likely to take a long time to load - if you lose patience you can click the **Stop** button.

e. Click here to see a choice of similar pages.

- Now type **marcasite** then click the **Google Search** button.

For this search, far fewer pages have been found, because "marcasite" is a far less common word than "crystals". The search engine is usually more useful than the directory for this type of search.

- This time, type **marcasite crystals** and start the search.

The search engine has found a huge number of pages this time, because it has found all the pages that contain the word "crystals" and all those that contain the word "marcasite".

- Now place these words in inverted commas ("marcasite crystals") and start a new search.

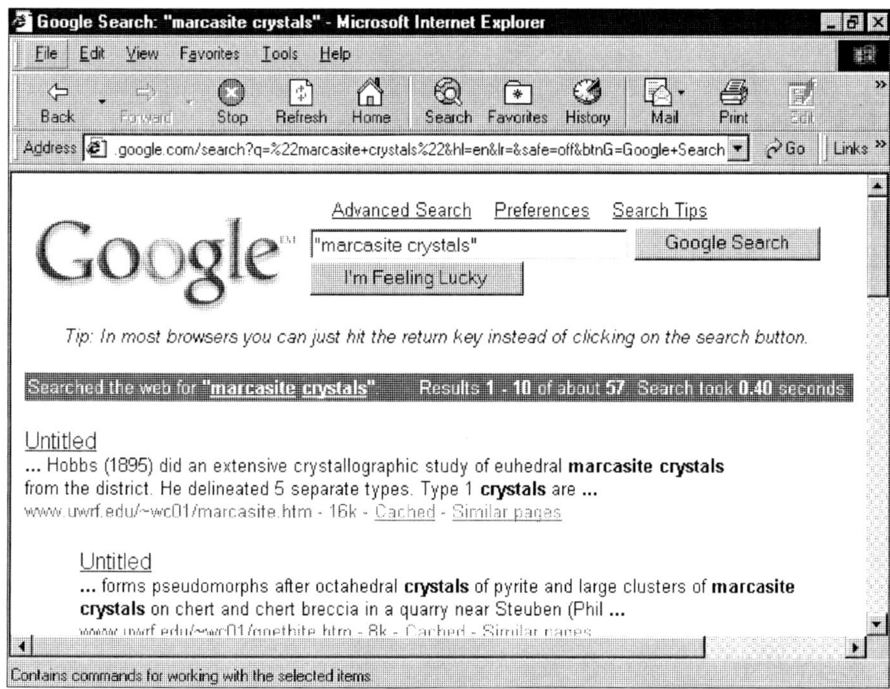

This search is far more precise, because the **engine** has chosen only those pages that contain the words "marcasite crystals".

Finding things on the Web

Most search engines that use an index allow you to specify advanced search criteria.

REFINING YOUR GOOGLE SEARCH

- Click the **Advanced Search** link next to the search text box.

  The search page now offers more options so that you can choose more precise criteria.

Google™ Advanced Search

Advanced Search Tips | All About Google

Advanced Web Search

Find results	with **all** of the words		10 results / Google Search
	with **any** of the words		
	with the **exact phrase**		
	without the words		
Occurrences	Return results where my terms occur	anywhere in the page	
Language	Return pages written in	any language	
Domains	Only return results from the site or domain	e.g. google.com, .org More info	
SafeSearch	No filtering / Filter using SafeSearch		

Page-Specific Search

Similar	Find pages similar to the page	Search (e.g. www.google.com/help.html)
Links	Find pages that link to the page	Search

Topic-Specific Search

Google offers specialized searches on the following topics:

Apple Macintosh - Search for all things Mac
BSD Unix - Search web pages about the BSD operating system
Linux - Search all penguin-friendly pages
U.S. Government - Search all .gov and .mil sites
Universities: Stanford, Brown, BYU, & more

Use the first zone in the page to give several keywords that should or should not be in the page you want:

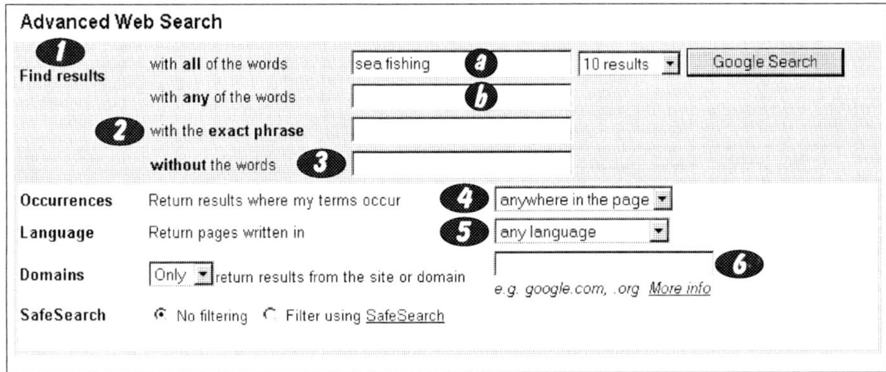

1. Type in the keywords.

    a. in this box if the pages should contain all the words you type.

    b. here if you want to find pages that contain any of the words.

2. If you want only pages that contain the exact phrase you have typed, enter it here.

3. Here you should type in any words you do not want to appear in the page. For example, if you are searching for recipes, but you do not like tomatoes, you could enter **recipes** in the first text box, and type **tomatoes** here.

4. If you like, you can specify where in the page the keywords should appear.

5. Choose the language you want.

6. If you want to, you can ask Google to find only pages from a given domain.

Finding things on the Web

- If you want to see a list of pages similar to a specific page, or that contain links to a specific page, type that page's address in the appropriate text box:

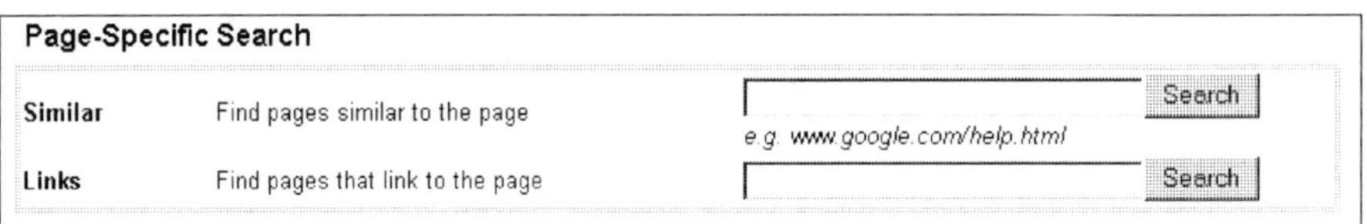

- When you have finished, click the **Google Search** button to start your search.

Of course, you do not have to fill out all the criteria in this page, but only those that correspond to your aims.

An index-based search engine will list Web pages containing pictures and sounds along with all the other pages matching your keyword. Some are helpful enough to let you search for them specifically.

SEARCHING FOR IMAGES, SOUNDS AND VIDEO CLIPS

- In some cases (the example below shows a site called Go.com), the options you need are next to the basic search text box:

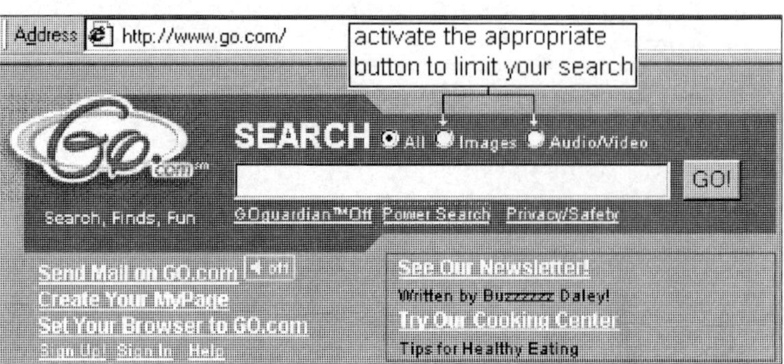

- Other search engines, such as Excite or Altavista (see the note in More search engine tips, below) provide links to specific **Images**, **MP3/Audio** or **Video** search pages. You may also find sites where these options appear on the advanced search page.

Now that you have a better understanding of search tools, you will already feel more comfortable with the Internet.

MORE SEARCH ENGINE TIPS

- Save search engines for the types of search they perform best, and remember that it is important to read the help pages for these tools. Doing this will save time in the long run, as your searches will be more efficient.
- Learning to use several tools of the same type is usually a waste of time.
- It is possible that, when you click on a result, the page behind it does not appear. In its place there is an error page (called Error 404). Also, the page you choose might not even contain your keyword! The most probable explanation for both these problems is to be found in the way the search engine's robots work. They read the pages at regular intervals, but the site designers may have changed the content in between times, making the search engine inaccurate until the next time a robot visits the site in question.
- Search engines let you carry out searches using **Boolean operators**: AND, OR, NOT etc...

  If you do not see straight away what these operators can be used for, here are some places to look for help.
- In Google, click the **Search Tips** link then go into **Basics** for a brief explanation.

Finding things on the Web

- The Altavista **Advanced Search** page starts with a **Boolean query** box: click **Help** for details.
  Altavista (http://www.altavista.co.uk) is the most sophisticated of the search engines. Try it out! Underneath its basic **Search for** text box is a **More Search Options** link, which gives you access to the equivalent of Google's advanced search. Once you have got to grips with these options, try the Altavista **Advanced Search**: start by reading the **Help** pages!

Below are some handy hints to help you avoid losing time on fruitless searches.

SEARCHING TECHNIQUES

- Choose the right tool for your search.
- Once you have started your search, try to analyse the first results and, if need be, change the keyword(s).
- If you still have not found what you want after about 15 minutes you should stop. It is possible that the subject you are searching is not on the Web. Try searching using discussion groups instead (see Part 4 in this book).
- It is a good idea to make a note of any sites that include links pages. These are like mini-directories specialised in the site's topic. Make use of this - somebody else has found all the good sites for you!

If you have trouble to begin with, do not despair. The Web is so complex that you could dedicate your career to trawling its millions of pages!

You will have noticed links on Web pages inviting you to write to the creators of the site or page. Maybe you have already clicked one of these links and found yourself in front of a blank page where you may or may not have written a message. This is e-mail, one of the principal Internet services, a service which allows you to receive messages and send them to anyone on the Internet, providing you know his or her e-mail address.

3rd Part

E-mail

Getting used to your e-mail tools

One of the most used services of the Internet is e-mail. It allows you to send messages to other people who are connected to the Internet, in only a few moments.

THE PRINCIPLE OF E-MAIL

- The principle of sending e-mail is as follows:

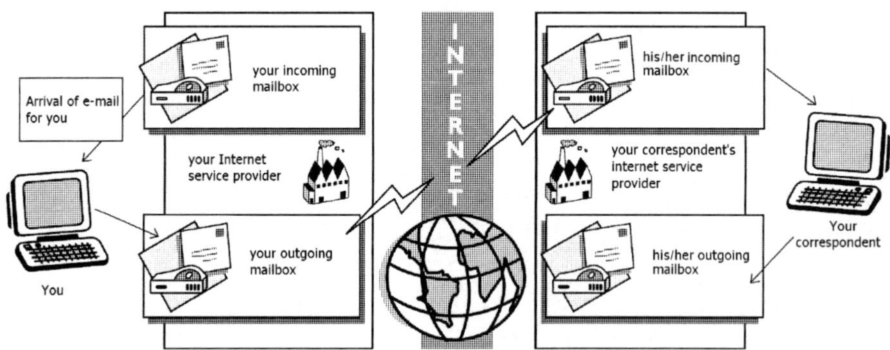

- When you send a message, it goes first to a computer that reads the recipient's address and sends it on in the right direction. This computer is your **SMTP server** or **outgoing mail server**, and it is responsible for managing your outgoing mail.
- When somebody sends you a message, it is stored on a computer, which saves all your messages until you connect to the Internet. This computer is your **POP server** (or possibly IMAP), or **incoming mail server**. It manages your incoming mailbox. POP stands for Post Office Protocol.
- Your ISP does not send you the contents of your mailbox as soon as you connect; **you need to collect your mail** by using the appropriate commands in your e-mail program.

Your correspondent does not need to be online before you can send him or her messages, because the messages will be stored in the incoming mailbox, on his/her ISP's server.
You should check your mailbox for messages frequently, otherwise it will be deleted after a given period of inactivity (this period depends on your ISP).

Do not confuse e-mail addresses (explained below) with Web addresses (which you saw in Part 2).

E-MAIL ADDRESSES

- You can recognise e-mail addresses because they contain the @ character.
- An e-mail address takes this form: user_name@server_name.

user_name this is the name or assumed name of the address' owner. It is often created using the first name (or initial) and surname of the person, which are sometimes separated with a hyphen or full stop. For example:
anne.watson@server_name
awatson@server_name
However, there are many variants!

@ a special character known as **at**.

server_name this identifies the computer that stores the mailbox.

- The server's name will depend on what sort of e-mail you have:
  - Mailbox with your ISP: anne.watson@serviceprovider.co.uk
  - Mailbox at your workplace: anne.watson@company.co.uk
  - Web-based mailbox (e-mail that you access by logging on to a Web site, offered by several sites such as Yahoo!, Hotmail.com, Lycos.co.uk): annewatson@yahoo.co.uk

This last type of e-mail can be useful for students, or for those who are often on the move, because you can check your e-mail from any computer.

  - E-mail transfer service: if you want to be able to change your ISP without having to change your e-mail address, get an address with a transfer service such as www.bigfoot.com. You will not have a mailbox with the service, but your messages will be redirected to the mailbox you specify: anne.watson@bigfoot.com

- Personal domain name: it is possible to buy a domain that you can then name after yourself, such as annewatson.com. Having created your own domain name, you can then create an e-mail address like messages@annewatson.com. You will have to pay for this privilege and prices vary. Go to sites such as www.domains.com or www.webnames.com for more information.

Many ISPs offer access to your mailbox via the Web as an extra service. This makes it possible to access your messages even if you are not at home, by going through the ISP's Web site.

You will find the same principal features in all e-mail applications. It is only if you are using a Web-based mailbox that you will have to get used to something a little different.

GETTING TO KNOW YOUR E-MAIL SOFTWARE

- First find the following in your program (or Web-based mailbox):

  a. The inbox.

  b. The messages you have sent.

  c. Messages that are ready to be sent.

  d. Draft messages.

  e. The waste bin (or trash).

In **Outlook Express**:

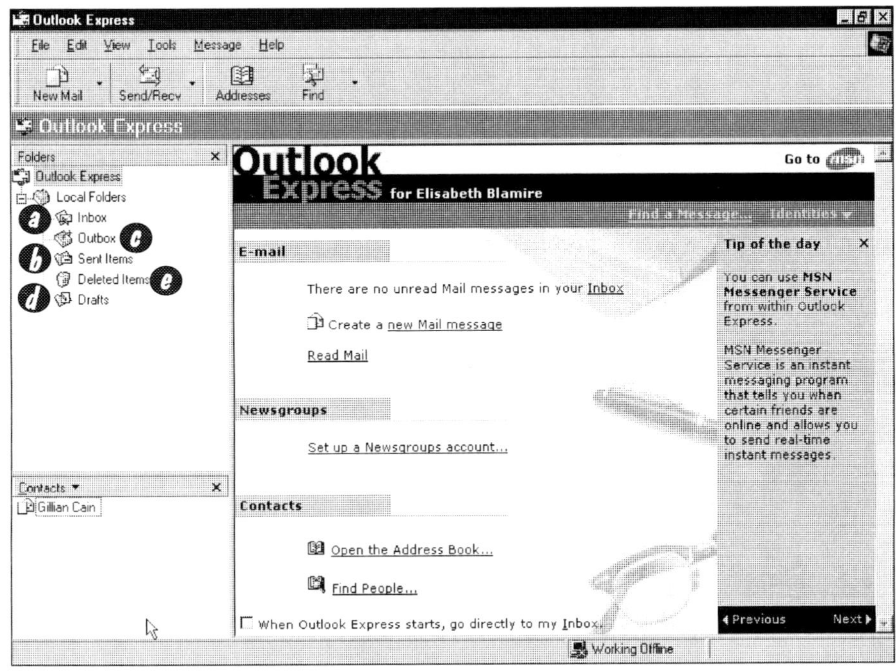

Getting used to your e-mail tools

- In **Netscape Messenger**:

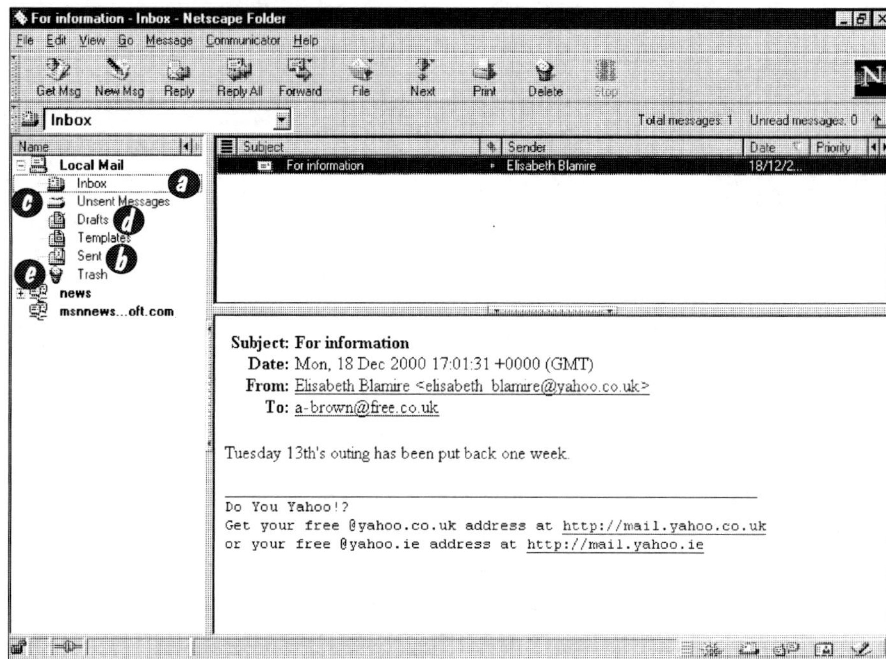

In **Yahoo!** Web-based mail:

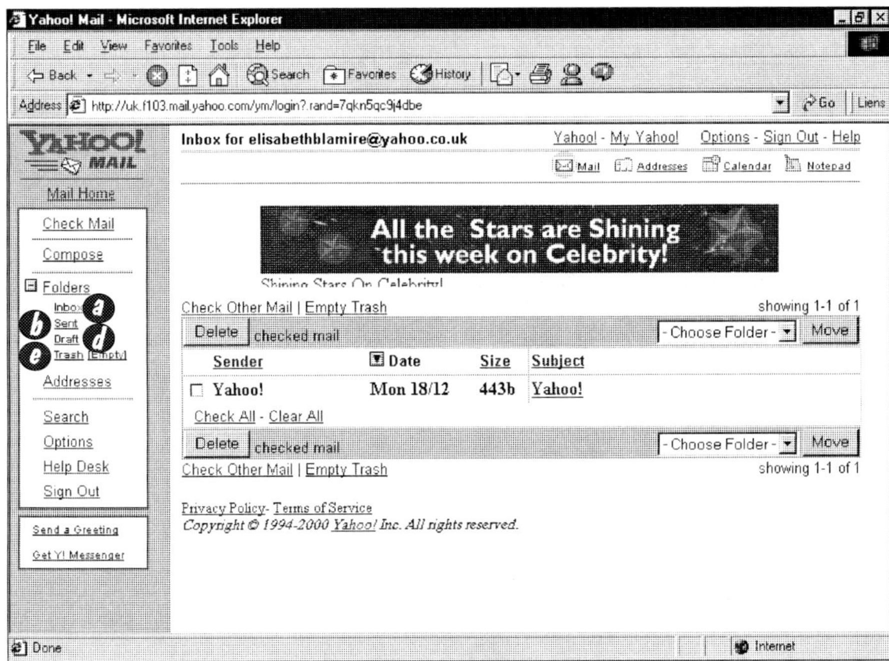

There is no outbox for unsent mail.

Dealing with messages

The techniques detailed in this chapter are based on the most popular free e-mail programs: Netscape Messenger and Outlook Express. Nevertheless, you should not have any trouble finding the equivalent commands in other e-mail software and Web-based e-mail.

SENDING A MESSAGE

Be careful here: your e-mail program needs to be correctly configured, which means that it needs to know the names of your incoming and outgoing mail servers, your e-mail address, and your name (your ISP supplies these: see also Part 1).

- Open your e-mail program.
- Click the **New Mail** (Outlook Express) or **New Msg** (Netscape Messenger) button.

A **New Message** window appears.

Outlook Express

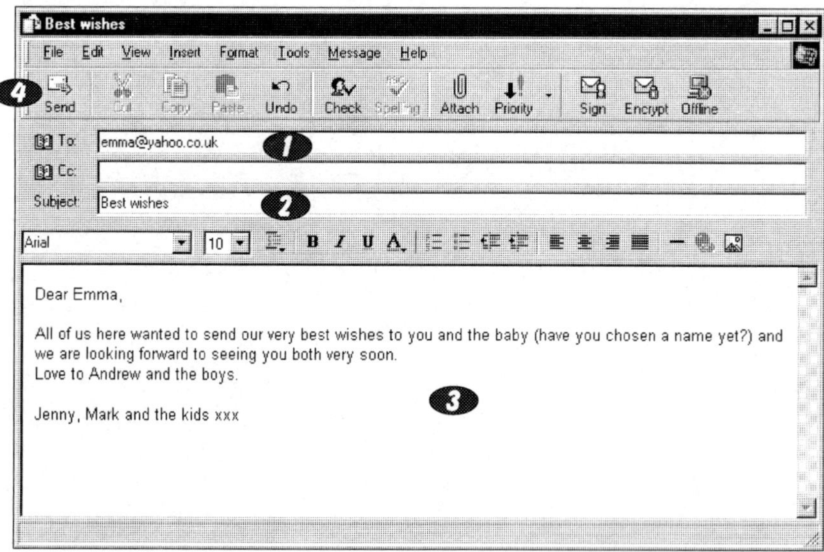

1. Type the recipient's address carefully: computers, unlike postmen, can only deliver messages if the address has been typed correctly. If you are sending the message to several people, separate the addresses with semi-colons.

2. Type in a few words to give the message a subject. This should resume the message contents and is important, because many people manage their incoming messages according to the subject.

3. The text of the message is entered here. You can write as much as you like.

4. Click this button to send the message.

Netscape Messenger

Once the message has been sent, it appears in the sent messages box.

It is a good idea to prepare all your messages offline. You should only connect to the Internet to send and receive messages, as this will keep your connection times short.

Dealing with messages

As shown in the diagram at the beginning of this section, you will need to ask the server to send your new e-mail messages to your computer before you can read them.

COLLECTING YOUR MAIL

Netscape Messenger

- Click the Get Msg button.

  This command will copy your messages onto your hard drive. You can disconnect as soon as you have finished.

- Now open the new mail folder: the **Inbox**.

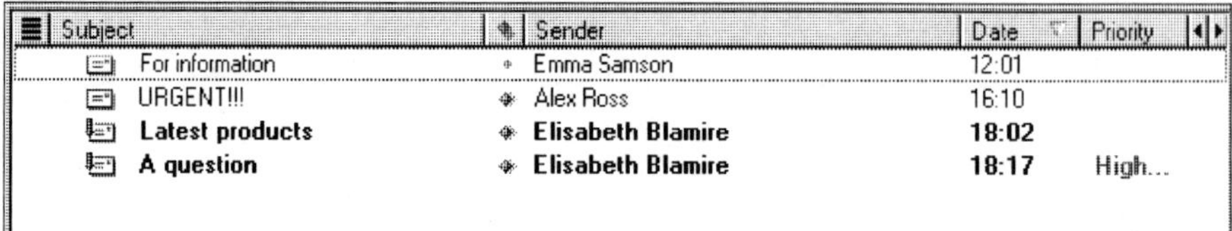

Subject	Sender	Date	Priority
For information	Emma Samson	12:01	
URGENT!!!	Alex Ross	16:10	
Latest products	**Elisabeth Blamire**	**18:02**	
A question	**Elisabeth Blamire**	**18:17**	High...

Notice that the sender's name and the subject identify the messages.

- Double-click a message to open it.

Outlook Express

- Click the **Send/Recv** button.

  This command will copy your messages onto your hard drive. You can disconnect as soon as you have finished.

- Now open the new mail folder: the **Inbox**.

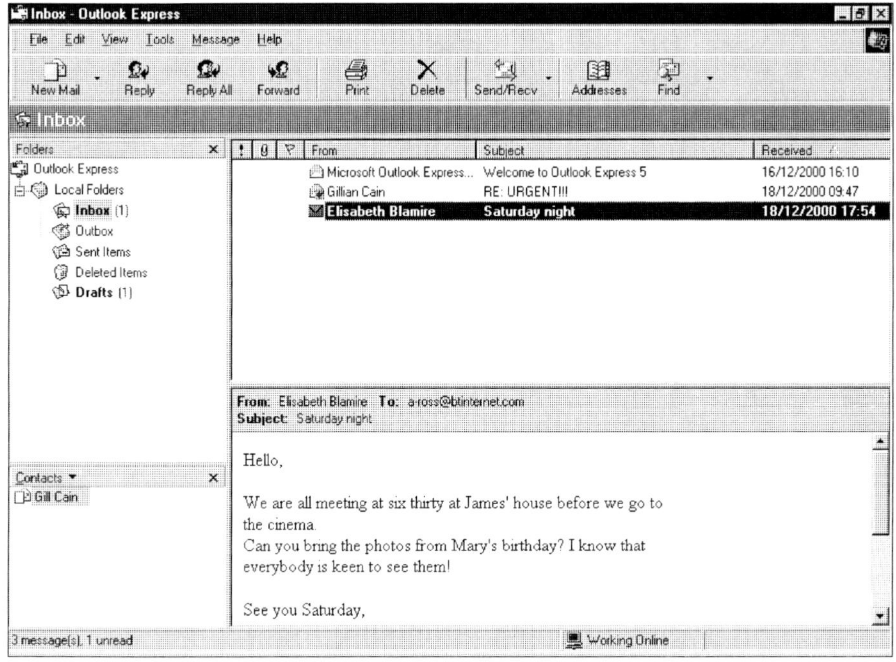

*You can see the **Contacts** pane underneath the **Folders** pane.*

- Double-click a message to read its contents.

  The message appears in a new window.

E-mail messages contain technical information, including the sender's e-mail address. By using this information, an e-mail program can produce a reply easily.

REPLYING TO A MESSAGE

- Select the message to which you want to reply.
- Click the **Reply** button.
- Use the message text box to write your reply. You can even insert your reply into the original message text, making sure to leave the characters that appear automatically to distinguish the messages.

Dealing with messages

Netscape Messenger

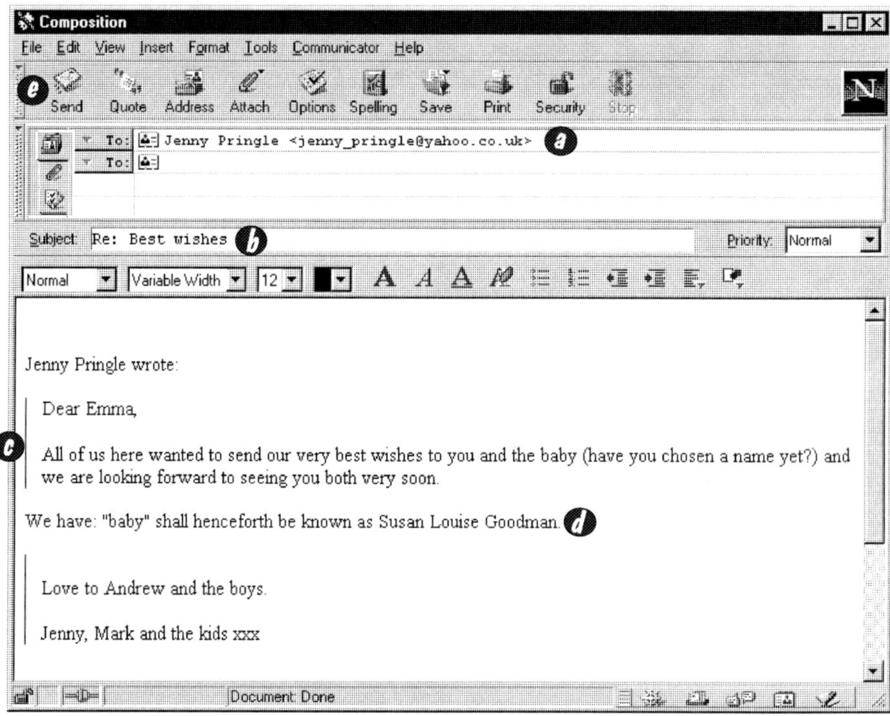

a. The recipient's address, which is the sender's address from the original message.

b. The subject of the original message, preceded by **Re** for reply.

c. The text of the original message. In Netscape Messenger, a line to the left marks this text.

d. The reply, which you can insert into the original text to create a "dialog".

e. Click this button to send the reply.

Outlook Express

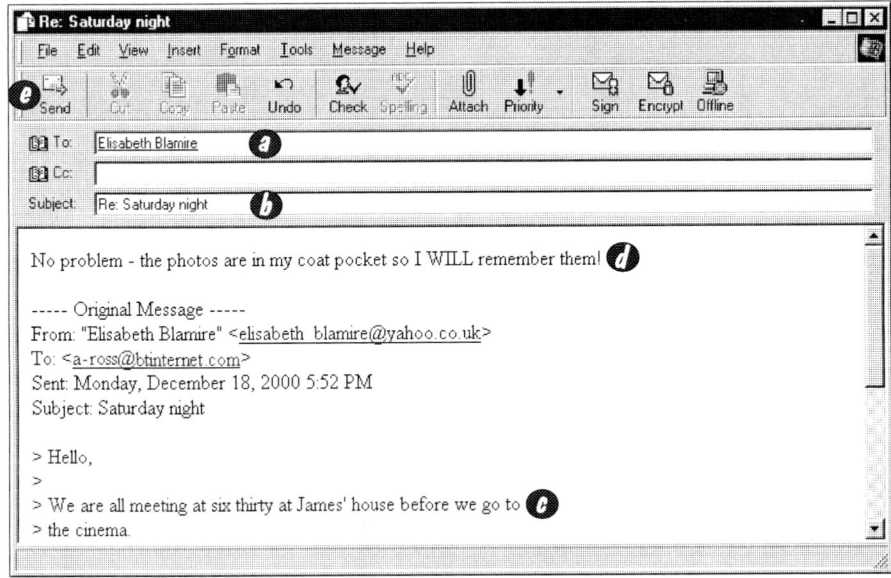

To avoid retyping your correspondents' addresses each time you send a new message and reduce the risk of errors, you can use your address book.

USING THE ADDRESS BOOK

Netscape Messenger

- Use the command given previously to create a new message.
- Do not fill in the address text box, but click the Address button.

Dealing with messages

The address book opens:

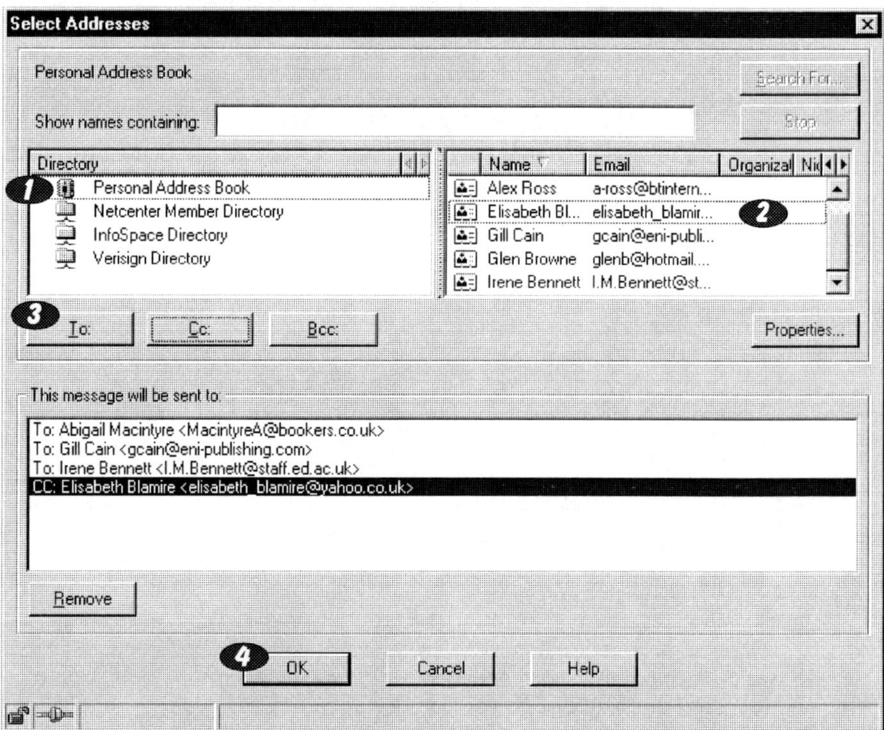

1. Select the address book you want to use.
2. Select the name of the recipient.
3. Click the **To:** button if the person is the main recipient, or **Cc:** to send a copy of the message to the person.
4. When you have finished, click **OK** to continue the message.

Outlook Express

- **View - Layout**: make sure that the **Contacts** option is active (ticked), and then click **OK**.

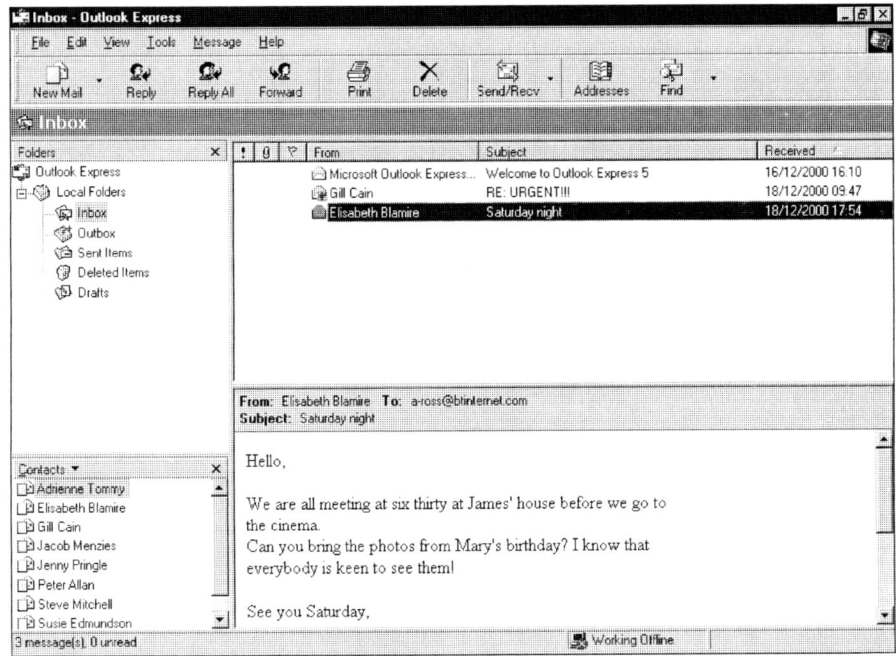

*You can see the **Contacts** pane below the **Folders** pane.*

- In the **Contacts** pane in the bottom left corner of the window, double-click the name of the person to whom you want to send a message.

  A New Message window appears, and it contains the address of the person you have just chosen.

- Fill in the **Subject** and type your message, then send it.

Dealing with messages

If you want to make the best use of the address book, you will obviously need to fill out all the addresses!

CREATING YOUR ADDRESS BOOK

Netscape Messenger

Communicator - Address Book

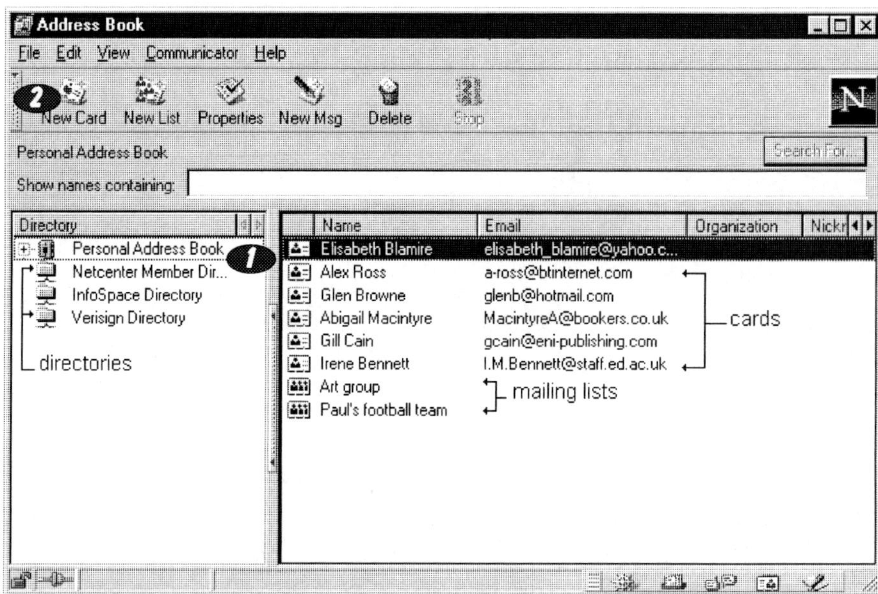

1. Select the **Personal Address Book**.
2. Choose to create a **New Card**.

E-mail

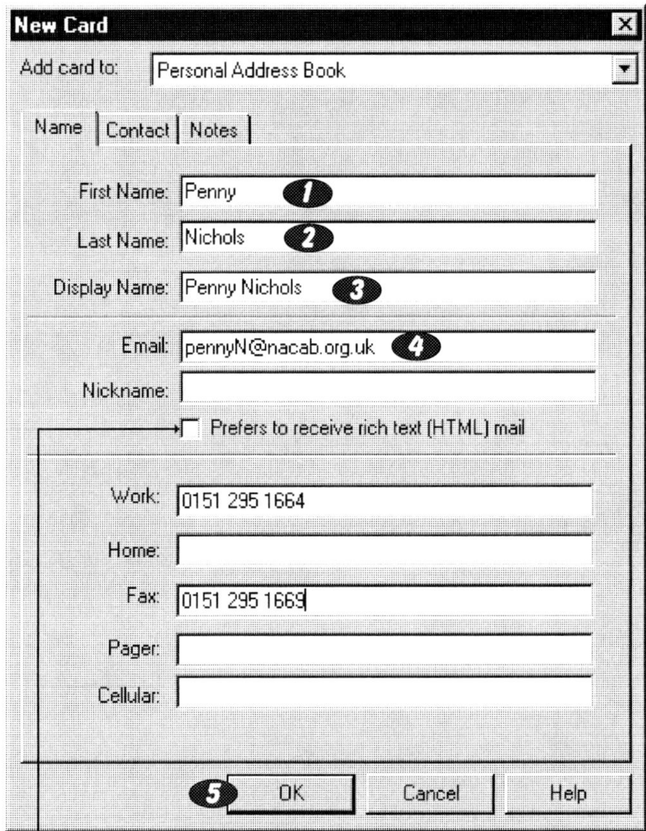

if this is not ticked, the message received will contain unformatted text

1. Give the **First Name**.
2. Type the **Last Name**.
3. If you want, change the **Display Name**.
4. Type in the **Email** address, being careful not to make any mistakes.
5. Click **OK**.

Dealing with messages

Outlook Express

- Click the Addresses button to go to the address book.

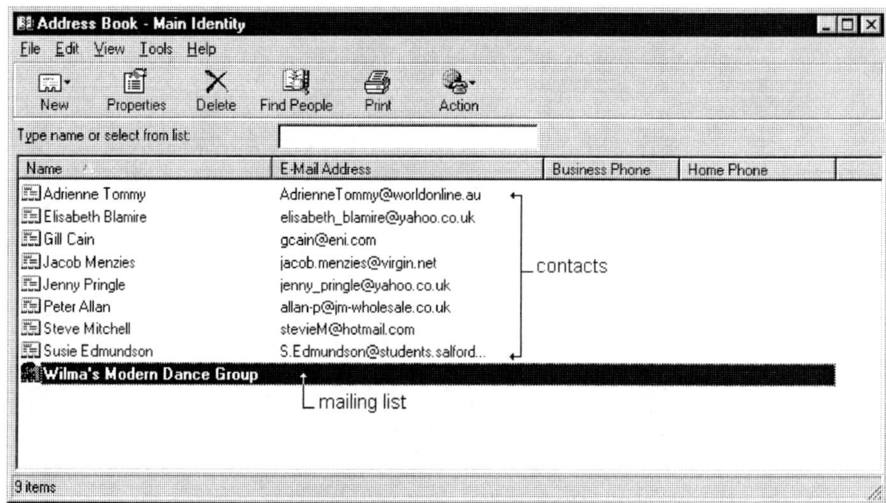

- **File - New Contact** or New

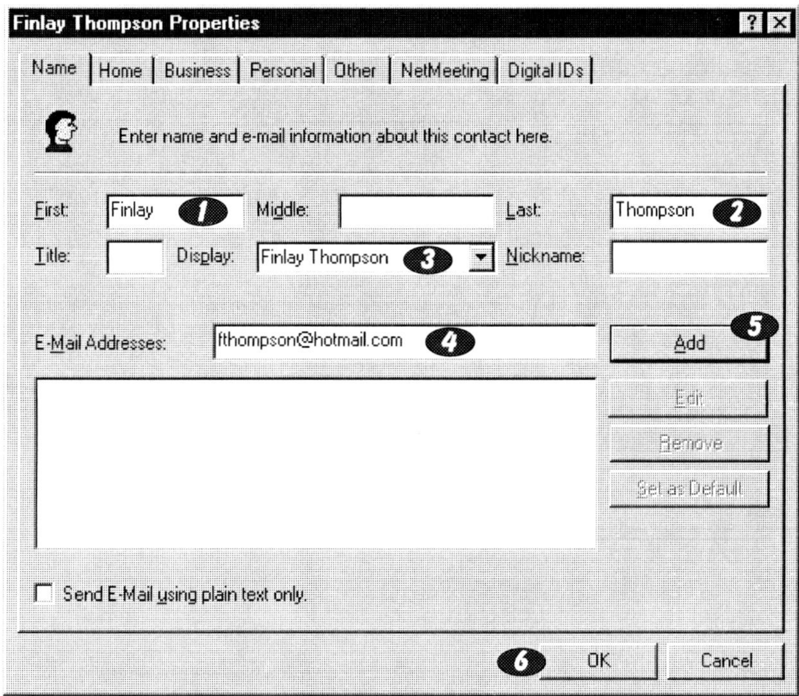

1. Give the person's **First** name.
2. Enter their **Last** name.
3. Change the name in the **Display** box, if you want.
4. Type in the E-mail address (without mistakes!).
5. Click the **Add** button.
6. Click **OK**.

When you receive a message from a new correspondent, you can add their address to your address book straight away:

- Click in the inbox to see the headers of the messages you have received.

Dealing with messages

- PC-users should right-click the message from the new correspondent, and Mac-users should hold the Ctrl key down whilst clicking the message.
- Click the **Add Sender to Address Book** option.

The address, which should be correct, is added to your address book.

Messages can, of course, contain text, but also documents (such as pictures, graphs, spreadsheets...) that have been joined to the message. For example, imagine that you are planning a family party and you want to send your menu ideas to your sister, who lives at the other end of the country. You can type out your ideas in Word (for example), then send them to your sister, who can make any changes she might think of. Once she has made her changes, she can return the Word file to you by e-mail, but also a list of all the guests in an Excel file. These documents are sent as attachments to your e-mails.

ATTACHED FILES (ATTACHMENTS)

- Write the message as shown previously.
- In Netscape Messenger, click the Attach button. Use the **Insert - File Attachment** command in Outlook Express.
- Select the file you want to attach to the message then click **Open** or **Attach**.
- Repeat these steps if you want to attach more files.
- Now send the message.

Watch out here: a message that is too big might delay other messages because the wires over which e-mail messages are sent are not designed for large data transfers. Some mail servers will block messages that are larger than 1 M, and you might receive a warning message if you frequently send cumbersome e-mails. If you have large files that you want to send over the Internet, you can always compress them before attaching them to messages, or you could use a different method to transfer your data, called FTP (see Part 5).

If your correspondent is to be able to read the files you have attached to your message, he or she will need to have a computer that is installed with the program you used to create the file. For example, if you have sent an Excel file, they will need to have Excel on their computer in order to be able to read the file. In the absence of the same program, the least they must have is a program that can read the format of the file you have sent. Some formats are "universal", and you should try to use these when creating documents that you want to send as e-mail attachments.

UNIVERSAL FILE FORMATS

- All e-mail messages have a fairly standard format, and so can be read by your correspondents, whatever e-mail program they happen to have.
- However, **attached files** are completely independent of e-mail programs, but simply accompany the message when it is sent. They are **completely dependent** on the program used to create them.
- Before you send an attachment to somebody, you should check that they have a program they can use to read your attachments. You should bear in mind the differences between PC and Mac operating systems. Fortunately, some file formats are more standard than others, and were created to be read by a large number of applications.
- For example, when you are sending **pictures**, you should always convert them to the JPEG format. This is because Web browsers can read this file format, so your correspondent will be able to read your file even if they do not have a graphics application.
- As for **sound** and **video** files, you should chose MPEG or QuickTime formats, as these can be read by the Windows Media Player or QuickTime (available for both Macs and PCs).
- The most common attachments are **text** files. For these sorts of document, try to use txt or rtf formats.

*Txt files are universal, but they do not support any formatting or tables, unlike **rtf** (**rich text format**), which is often a better choice.*

SAVING A WORD FILE IN RTF FORMAT

This format is recognised by all versions of Word, on PCs and Macs, and by all other word processing applications. This makes it a particularly good choice as the format of attached text files.

- Create your file and, when you come to save it, use the **File - Save As** command.

The following dialog box appears:

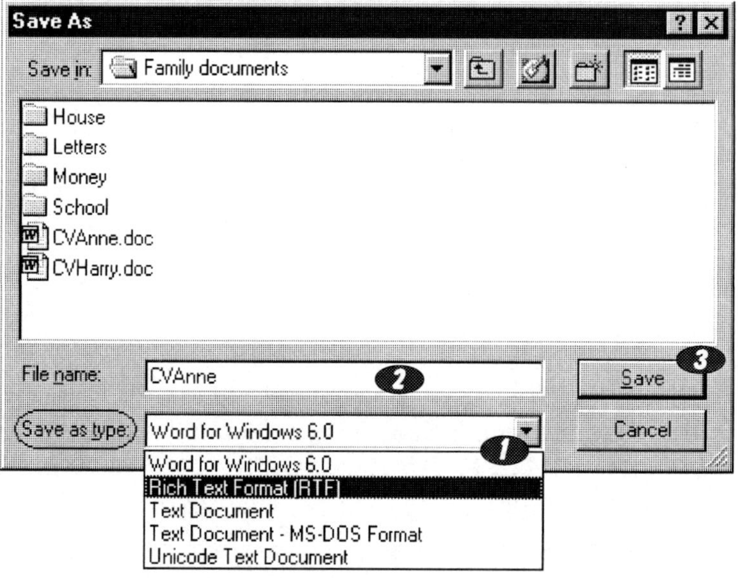

1. In the **Save as type** drop-down menu, choose **Rich Text Format (RTF)** or any format with the extension RTF.
2. Give the file a name.
3. Save the file.

In Windows, you will obtain a file with the **.rtf** extension, described as a **Rich Text Format** file, or possibly a **Formatted text** file.

CVAnne.doc	20 KB	Microsoft Word Document
CVAnne.rtf	15 KB	Rich Text Format

Lists

One way to be sure to receive messages on a regular basis is to subscribe to a list (mailing list or discussion list).

MAILING LISTS

- **Mailing lists** are explained in this section because they are managed in the same way as e-mail. To receive messages from a mailing list, you have to subscribe to the list. In simple terms, your e-mail address is sent to a computer and every time a new issue of the list's newsletter is created, the computer sends a copy to your address automatically.
- Some mailing lists are free, others charge for the service, some are open to all-comers and others have membership restrictions (such as your profession, or membership of a society).
- As you surf the Internet, you will certainly come across sites that offer subscription to their mailing list. For example, if you go to www.learnthenet.com, you can subscribe to a weekly newsletter destined for new users of the Internet:

- If you want to unsubscribe from a service, each issue of the newsletter has details of the unsubscription procedure, which requires only a few clicks.

Discussion lists are often confused with discussion groups (forums), because both media enable members to exchange information with each other (discussion groups are explained in Part 4 of this book).

DISCUSSION LISTS

- Mailing lists, which send you newsletters, work in one direction only.
- Discussion lists are, technically, sent in the same way as newsletters, but are different because each member receives all the messages sent to the list and can participate in debates by sending his or her own messages to the other list members.
- To avoid enormous numbers of e-mail circulating, most lists are controlled. Someone takes care of filtering messages sent to the list and only sends them on to the list if the message contents are relevant.

The Internet provides you with various means of discussing any given topic with a group of total strangers, or a chosen circle of correspondents. Much cheaper and less intrusive than the telephone, these new communication channels will convince many people of the advantages of the Internet revolution.

4th Part

Internet discussion and chat

Discussion forums

Even if you are new to the Internet, you have probably already heard of forums, newsgroups and discussion groups, which are destined for the exchange of ideas about a given subject. To avoid confusion, here is an explanation of exactly what a forum is.

DEFINING FORUMS

- This Internet service goes by many different names: newsgroups, discussion groups, discussion forums etc...

  The term forum will be used in this book.

- Forums can be compared to a collection of rooms. In each room the conversation is based on a given subject. The code of conduct is called the **forum charter**.
- You can enter the rooms via a news program and a simple subscription process.
- In these rooms, messages are "displayed" ("posted" is the common term), with only the first few words visible (the message header). Click the header to see the whole text and the author's e-mail address.
- Messages in the forum can be accessed, using a news program, for about two weeks.
- A Web-user can:
  - visit the forum to read the messages,
  - read messages then reply to the author, without leaving their "trace" in the forum,
  - make their reply public in the forum,
  - or post a message, in compliance with the forum's rules, of course.

A forum's address will usually indicate what its theme is.

UNDERSTANDING FORUM ADDRESSES

- Forum addresses have evolved as they have developed. The first users laid down the basic structures for naming different subjects, as follows:
  - sci for sciences
  - rec for recreational subjects
  - misc for miscellaneous forums.
- As the number of forum-users has grown, users in different countries have created their own groups for their country. For example, British users have created the uk. prefix, indicating forums destined for UK-users.
- In the ever-expanding world of forum-use, the uk.rec forum became much too cumbersome, because the subject was too vague, so more forums on the same theme have been created, such as:
  - uk.rec.aquaria.misc,
  - uk.rec.birdwatching,
  - uk.rec.climbing,
  - uk.rec.gardening,
  - uk.rec.motorcycling,
  - uk.rec.sailing,

  the subjects of which are obvious.

Discussion forums

The **www.deja.com** site (see below) is full of useful information about forums, and includes a directory of hundreds of groups you can visit and try. It also has information for people who are new to the world of forums, with advice on how to subscribe, post messages and even on creating your own forum.

It is a good idea to have a look at the **FAQ**s (Frequently Asked Questions) when you visit a forum. There you will find the answers to the most commonly posed questions about the forum, compiled by the forum's regular users. Getting to know more about the forum in this way will help you fit in more easily, and keeps questions out of the forum discussion, making the "conversation" flow more freely.

Before you decide to subscribe, you should first read through a forum to get an idea of the content.

SEARCHING FOR INFORMATION IN A FORUM

- As mentioned previously, articles posted to forums are only available for two weeks or so and are accessible using a news program.
- However, you can consult the archives of a forum:
  - before you subscribe, to have a better idea which one to choose,
  - if you want to find out what has been said about a company, a product, or perhaps find an expert-opinion about something.
- There are several specialised tools that archive all the contents of forums and allow you to keep track of what has been said and by whom. The best known is on the **http://www.deja.com** site.

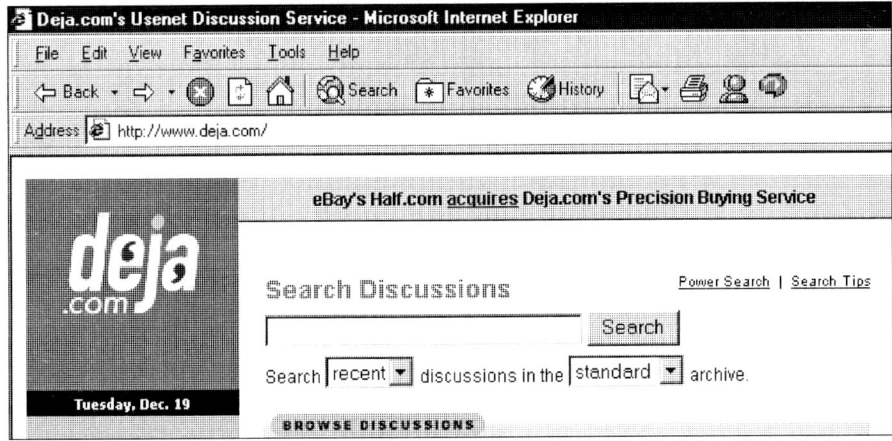

- On the site's homepage - which is ever changing in its appearance - look for the search banner.

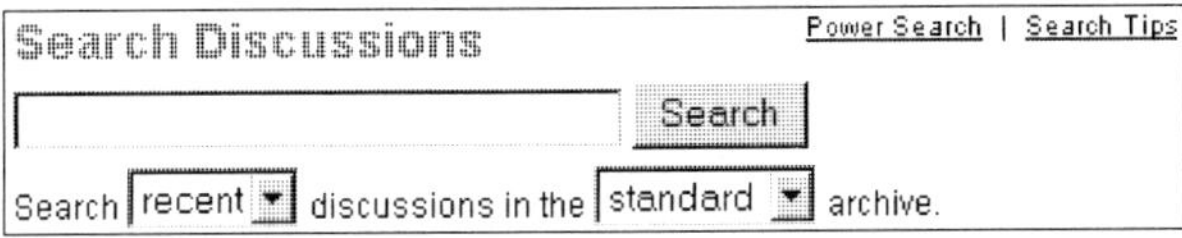

- Click the **Power Search** link.

This leads you to a very efficient search interface:

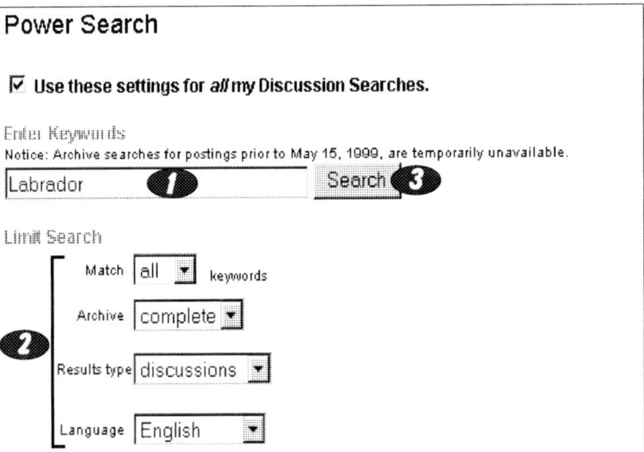

1. Enter your keywords.

2. Use these options to refine your search.

3. Start searching by clicking here.

In the result pages you will find messages that contain your keywords, the authors' e-mail addresses and the names of the forums in which the messages were posted. This should give you a much better idea of which forums you want to join.

Once you have decided which forum you want to join, all you have to do is join!

JOINING FORUMS

- Even though you can find software that is dedicated for use with forums (such as FreeAgent freeware), both Outlook Express and Netscape Messenger include a module you can use to access forums. The first thing you need to do is to add a news server.

Adding a news server in Outlook Express

This software uses the term **newsgroup** instead of forum. You must add your news server to your e-mail program if you want to be able to participate in the forums. Your ISP will have given you the address of its news server.

- **Tools - Accounts**

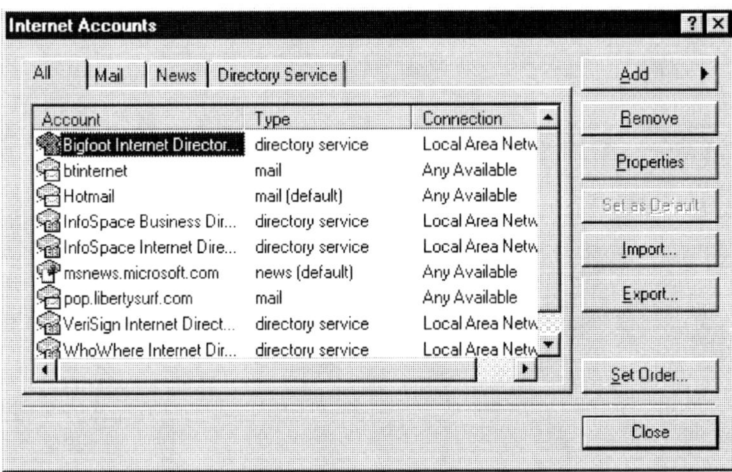

*The **Internet Accounts** dialog box appears. You can see the **Directory Services** (for finding people or businesses), the **Mail** servers (which you use to access your e-mail account) and the **News** servers.*

- Click the **Add** button and choose the **News** option.
- Give your **Display name** (the name or alias you want to use to participate in forums) then click **Next**.
- Type your **E-mail address** and click **Next**.
- Enter the **News (NNTP) server** your ISP gave you.
- Click **Next** then **Finish**.

The server now appears in the Internet Accounts box, in the All tab and also in the News tab.

- Click **Close**.

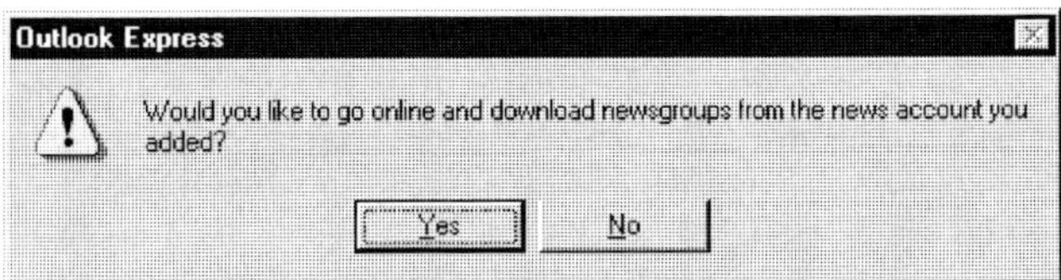

Outlook Express will ask you if you want to connect to the Internet (if you are working offline) and download the news server's forums.

Discussion forums

- Click **Yes** if you want to download the forums, or **No** if you want to do it later.

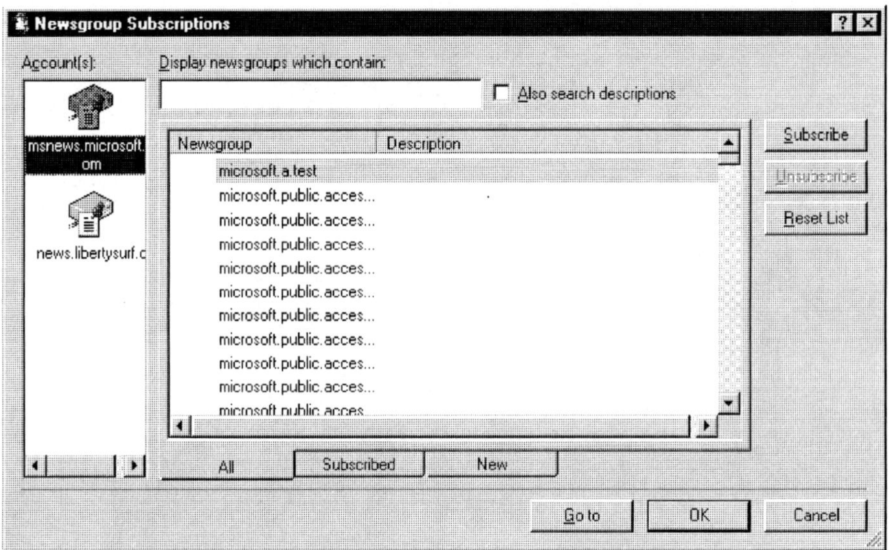

*If you choose to download the newsgroups, the **Downloading** dialog box appears. This process may take a few minutes, but you only need to do it once. After the newsgroups have been downloaded, the **Newsgroup Subscriptions** dialog box appears.*

- Now you can subscribe to the forums of your choice (see below), or visit one. Simply click the name of the forum then click **Go to**.

The next time you run Outlook Express, this group will no longer be visible in the folder list. If you want it to be visible all the time, you will need to subscribe to the forum (see below).

Subscribing to a forum in Outlook Express

This procedure lets you include forums in your folders list, so that you can access them easily, or read them while you are offline.

- If necessary, open the **Newsgroup Subscriptions** dialog box using **Tools - Newsgroups**.
- Click the news server you want to use, then the group you want to join. If you cannot see the full name of each group, drag the right border of the **Newsgroup** column header.
- Click the **Subscribe** button.

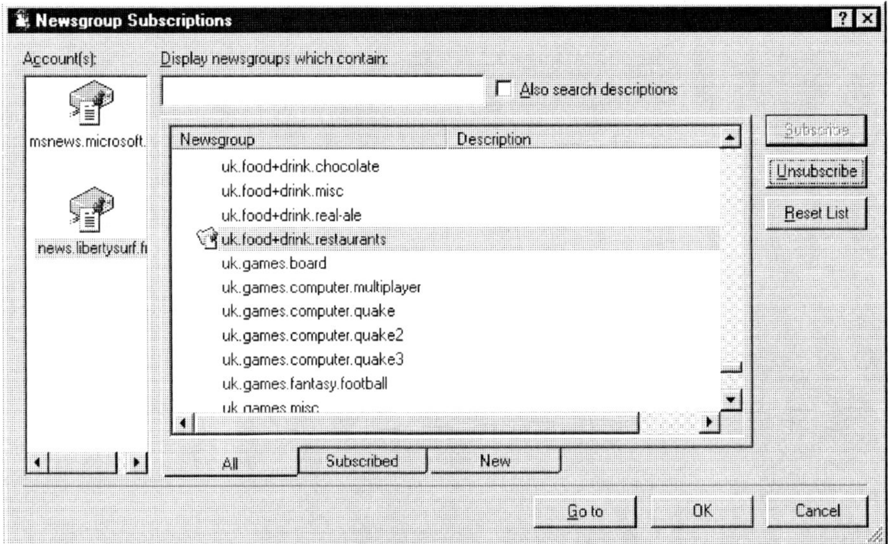

A symbol appears before the group's name.

- Click **Go to** to close the dialog box and see the contents of the newsgroup you have chosen.

Be patient, and watch the status bar while you are waiting. Outlook Express connects to the group and tells you how many read and unread messages there are and how many have not been downloaded. If your status bar shows the information below, the newsgroup does not contain any messages.

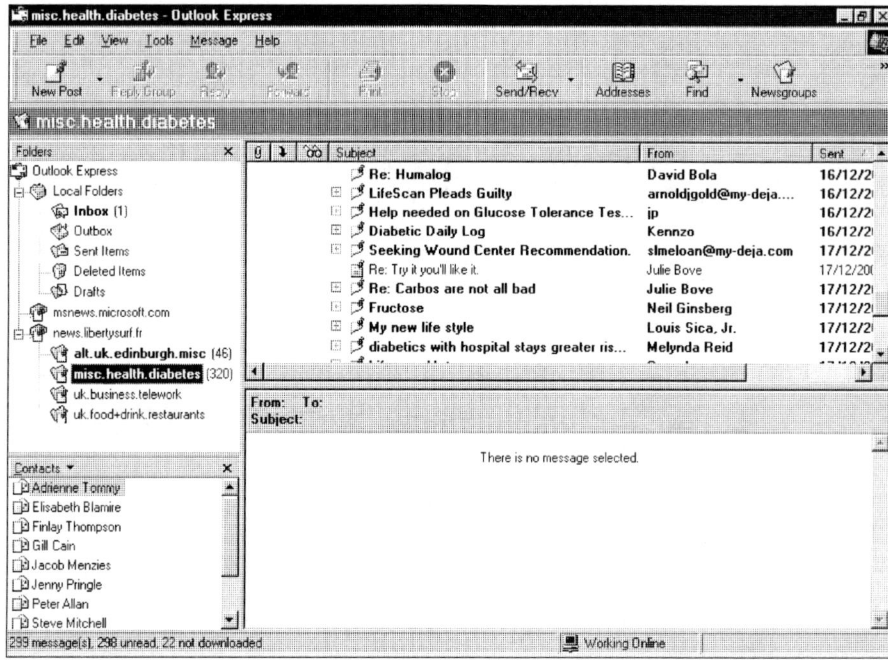

The dialog box closes and you can see the messages in the group. The symbol that precedes the group's name is coloured, because you have subscribed to the group (otherwise, it would be grey).

To unsubscribe from a forum, select it and click the **Unsubscribe** button in the **Newsgroup Subscriptions** dialog box (accessible via **Tools - Newsgroups**).

Adding a news server in Netscape Messenger

You must add your news server to your e-mail program if you want to be able to participate in the forums. Your ISP will have given you the address of its news server.

- **Edit - Preferences**
- If necessary, click the "+" sign next to the **Mail & Newsgroups** category.
- Activate the **Newsgroup Servers** category.

- Click the **Add** button.

1. Give the name of your ISP's news server (or the news server you want to add).
2. If necessary, change the port number used by your news server. 119 is the most commonly used number.
3. Activate this option if you want to send and receive encoded messages. If you choose this option, only people who know your key will be able to read your messages. You are not advised to activate this option, because forums are public.
4. If you want to give your username and password each time you go to a forum, activate this choice.
5. Click **OK**.

- If necessary, click the **Set as Default** button.

If you want to remove a news server, click it then press the Del key and confirm the deletion. You cannot make any changes to news server names, so if you make a mistake you will have to delete the server and start again.

Discussion forums

Subscribing to a forum in Netscape Messenger

Once you have added the news server, you need to subscribe before you can consult the forums.

- In Netscape Messenger's main window, click the name of the news server your ISP gave you.
- **File - Subscribe**

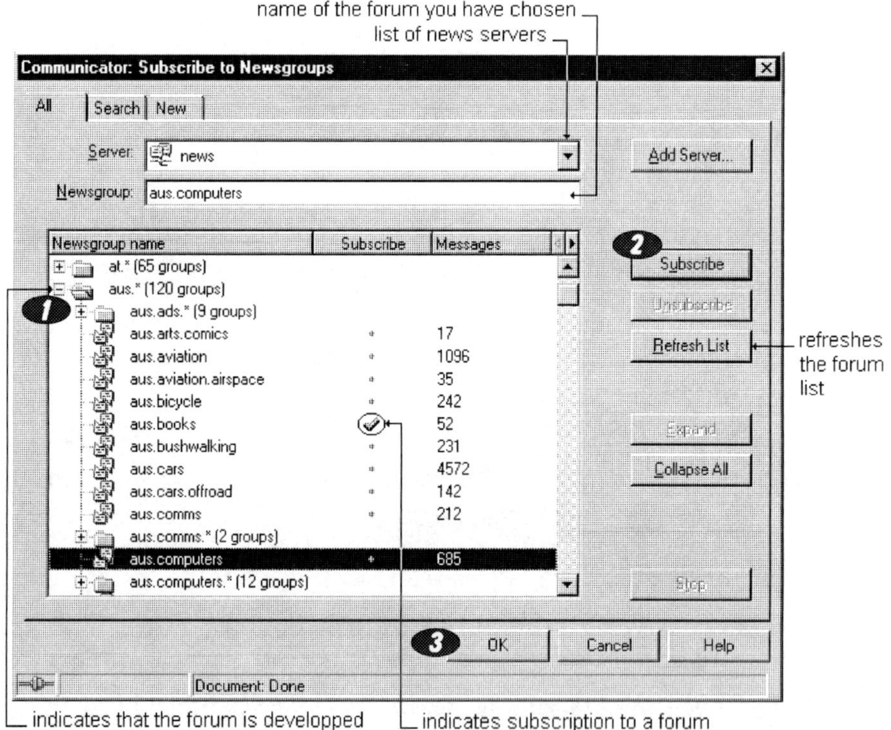

1. If you need to, expand the list by clicking the "+" sign.
2. Subscribe to the forum you want by clicking the mark or the **Subscribe** button.
3. Click **OK**.

To see the forum messages, go to the main Netscape Messenger window, or the Message Center and double-click the forum's name.

If the forum contains more than 500 messages, and depending on the server's configuration, the following dialog box might appear.

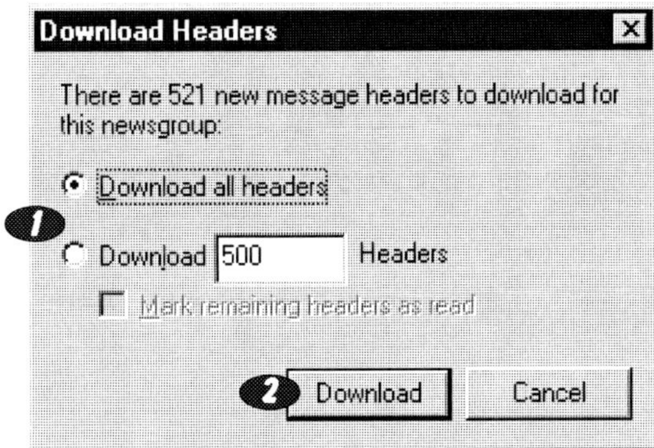

1. Select the first option if you want to download all the messages. If you do not, activate the second option and specify how many messages you want to download.
2. Start downloading.

Discussion forums

The message headers appear in the Messenger window. Read the forum messages in the same way as you read e-mail messages:

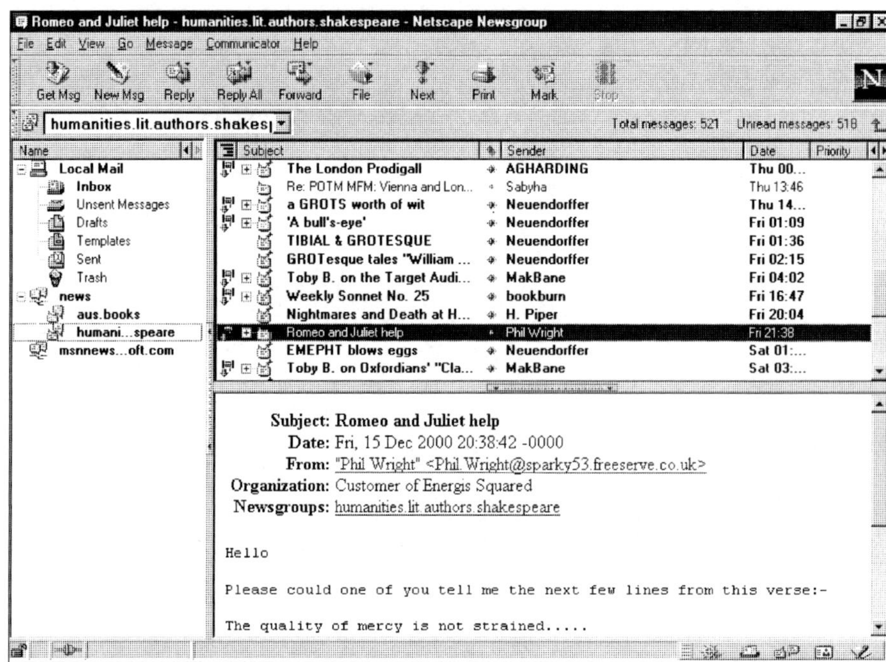

Easier to use, but often not very active, Web message boards are an alternative.

WEB MESSAGE BOARDS

- Some Web sites include one or more message boards. You can access them through your Web browser and they are completely different from the forums described previously. The site owner is solely responsible for the content and traffic in the message board. Below you can see a message from one of the boards on the ivillage UK site.

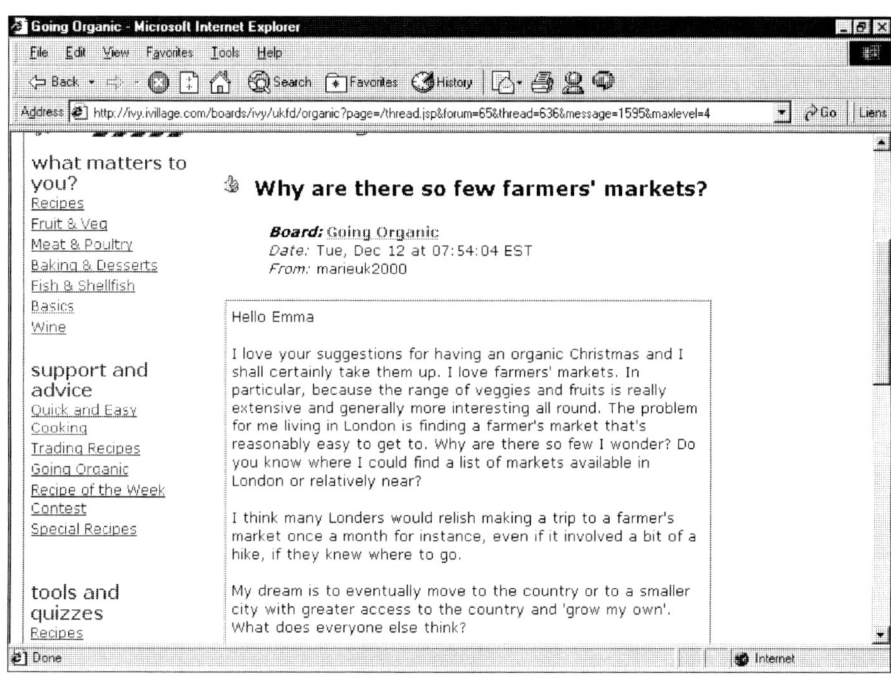
Going Organic - Microsoft Internet Explorer
File Edit View Favorites Tools Help
Back Search Favorites History
Address http://ivy.ivillage.com/boards/ivy/ukfd/organic?page=/thread.jsp&forum=65&thread=636&message=1595&maxlevel=4
Go Liens
what matters to you?
Recipes
Fruit & Veg
Meat & Poultry
Baking & Desserts
Fish & Shellfish
Basics
Wine
support and advice
Quick and Easy Cooking
Trading Recipes
Going Organic
Recipe of the Week Contest
Special Recipes
tools and quizzes
Recipes
Why are there so few farmers' markets?
Board: Going Organic
Date: Tue, Dec 12 at 07:54:04 EST
From: marieuk2000
Hello Emma
I love your suggestions for having an organic Christmas and I shall certainly take them up. I love farmers' markets. In particular, because the range of veggies and fruits is really extensive and generally more interesting all round. The problem for me living in London is finding a farmer's market that's reasonably easy to get to. Why are there so few I wonder? Do you know where I could find a list of markets available in London or relatively near?
I think many Londers would relish making a trip to a farmer's market once a month for instance, even if it involved a bit of a hike, if they knew where to go.
My dream is to eventually move to the country or to a smaller city with greater access to the country and 'grow my own'. What does everyone else think?
Done
Internet

Live chat

Chat is a live, online conversation, carried on through a software interface.

CHATTING ON THE WEB

- The easiest way to chat is to go to a chat "room" in a Web site. Try these examples:
  http://uk.chat.yahoo.com, where there is a large choice of topics
  or
  http://chat.msn.co.uk, which has the advantage of being very easy to use.

  Once you have clicked on the chat room you want to visit, a chat tool will be installed on your computer automatically, or a dialog box will ask you if you want the software installed, depending on the chat service you are using.

- After this, you will be asked to give an alias, or sign in. Then you can start to chat. When you leave the chat, the chat tool will be removed from your computer.

If you would like to chat more, go ahead and install IRC tools. This may be a more technical choice, but offers more possibilities.

INSTALLING IRC TOOLS

- IRC stands for Internet Relay Chat, a technique that exists since the Internet's early days in 1985.
- Before you can access IRC channels, you first need to download and install specialist software: **Mirc** for PC users or **Ircle** if you have a Mac.
- When you start this program, you will have to enter your name and e-mail address and give a nickname. You will also have to choose which server you want to log on to, but for the first use, the default server will suffice.
- The server now displays a list of all the available channels. Their names appear as #name.

  Often, the name of the channel is fairly explicit and you can guess at the chat conversation topic fairly accurately.

- If you want to join a chat, choose the one that interests you. You may have to choose another **nickname** if the one you choose originally is already taken. And now you can join the chat.

If you want to chat often, it is best to learn some of the language used by the Internet community.

DISCOVERING IRC LANGUAGE

- IRC is a world of its own on the Internet. The rules of conduct are not unlike those for forums: no insults, leave if you do not like it and no advertising.
- You talk to others using your keyboard and so a lot of the language is phonetic or symbol-based shorthand. For instance: ":-) 2 cu" means "Pleased to see you".
- You will notice some "codes" in use:
  - **kicked**: asked to leave for inappropriate behaviour.
  - **banned**: excluded from the channel.
  - **op**: the person who is responsible for making sure the channel is working correctly.
- These are some basic commands you must know:
  - **/join**: if you want to join a channel.
  - **/part**: to leave the current channel.
  - **/nick "nickname"**: to change your nickname.

You can choose to chat with a few select people by using an instant messaging service.

CHATTING IN A PRIVATE GROUP

- Live online chatting in a private group is known as **instant messaging**.
- Everybody in the discussion needs to have the same free software (freeware) installed on his or her computer. At the moment, these programs are not inter-compatible, but they should be soon.

Live chat

- The functions and tools are mostly similar:
    - a list of your "friends" (the people you chat with the most) is displayed in a small window on your screen.
    - you can see which of your friends is online at any given time.
    - you have a one-to-one conversation, or a discussion with several people.
- The most common instant messaging tools are:
    - **AIM (AOL Instant Messenger)**: available to all Internet users, no matter who their ISP is. Download it from: **http://www.aol.co.uk/messenger**.

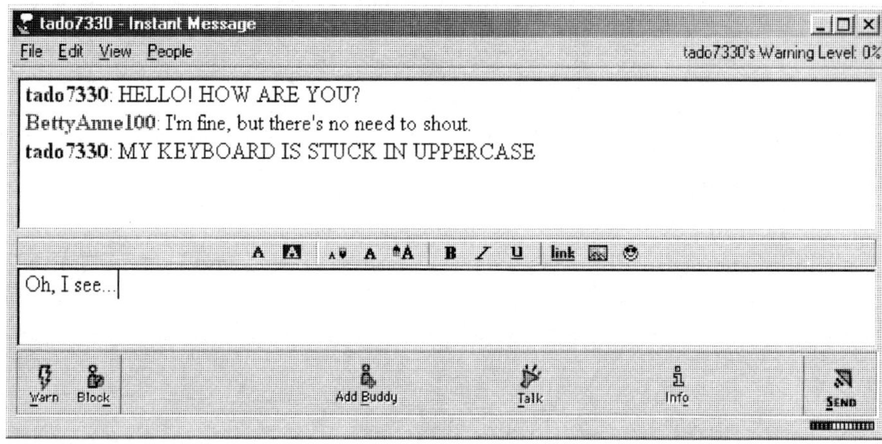

- **ICQ** (pronounced I seek you). Download it from: **http://www.icq.com**

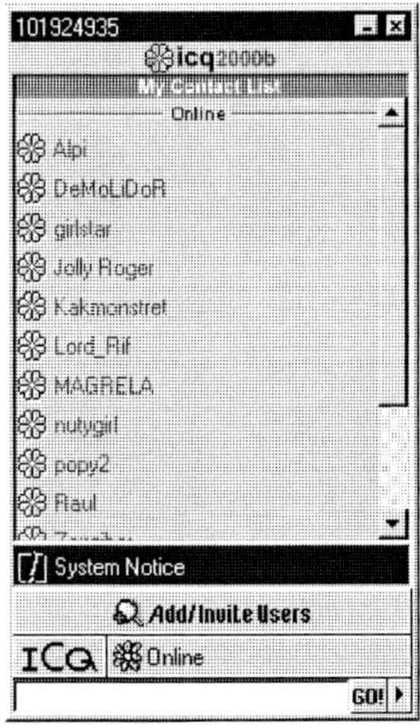

You communicate using your keyboard.

- **Yahoo! Messenger**, an excellent newcomer. To download it, go to: **http://uk.yahoo.com**

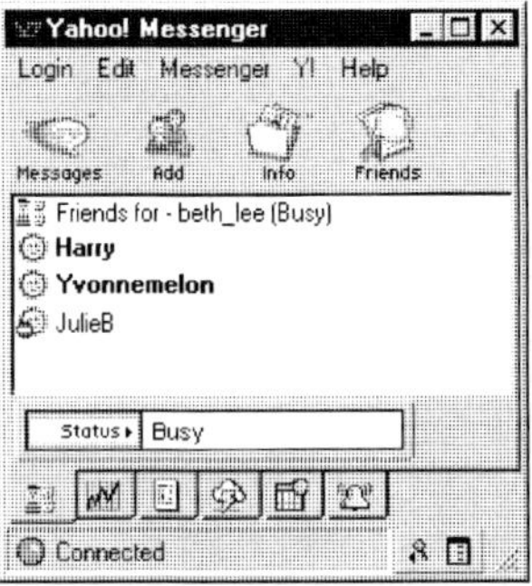

This tool includes a **Voice Chat** facility, which you can use to talk to anyone, anywhere in the world, without worrying about the telephone costs, because all you pay is your Internet connection. You can converse via your keyboard or using a microphone (obviously, your correspondents will need to have speakers to hear what you have to say).

Webcams

This technique involves connecting a small camera (a Webcam) to your computer so that you and your correspondents can see each other whilst you are communicating (providing your correspondents have webcams too!). Remember that a Webcam is not like a camcorder - it needs to be connected to your computer before it will work.

WEBCAMS

Description

- A webcam is not a camcorder. It cannot record, but simply captures fixed or moving images. It has to be connected to a computer in order to work.
- This is the important technical information:
  - **The camera's resolution**: this will determine the picture quality. The current market-standard is 100 000 pixels.
  - **The image size**: 352 x 288 pixels corresponds to a quarter of your computer screen, and 640 x 480 pixels will provide an image at nearly full-screen size.
  - **The speed**: for good quality moving pictures, the webcam should be able to handle at least 25 frames per second.
- The most basic models cost around £30 - £35, but for better value for your money, you should look to pay about £50.

Webcam uses

- **Video-conferencing**: all the participants' computers must be equipped with a webcam, a microphone and the same video-conferencing software. The most common freeware is **Microsoft Net-Meeting** (included with Internet Explorer). Everybody needs to have a good connection (such as ISND or ADSL). Wherever in the world the participants are, they will only pay for the Internet connection.
- Several sites contain a live image from a webcam, which is updated regularly. You can see any number of things in this way, such as the sunset in Singapore or the private life of Miss Z in Los Angeles. There are more and more webcams on the Web, but also directories to help you find interesting ones. Try **http://www.camcentral.com**.

In spite of the rather uninviting technical ring of these two terms, this section is about an Internet service which will open exciting new avenues in the use and enjoyment of your computer and solve many little problems for you.

5th Part

Downloads/compression

Download services

In Part 3 you learned that e-mail is no good if you want to send large files. If you want to swap images and videos, or download software onto your hard drive, you will need to use a different network, that works with FTP (File Transfer Protocol).

THE DOWNLOAD NETWORK

- This network which, like e-mail and the Web, is part of Internet's services, enables you to send any files, no matter how big.

  You will often use it without realising. For instance, every time you download software from a Web site, you are using FTP.

Anyone can copy software from the Internet onto their own computer. You are sure to get the right result if you just follow the download links, even if you are not a software expert.

Some sites include a great number of animations and videos. In order to be able to view these effects, you will need a specific program called a plug-in. Plug-ins are designed to work with browsers. They add extra functions that were not included when the browser was designed. Below you can find out about the most common plug-ins.

PLUG-INS

- Sometimes, when you register with an ISP, plug-ins are included in the connection CD-ROM you received. If this is the case, go ahead and install them to get the most out of the animated Web.
- This said, plug-ins are constantly evolving and being updated, so you will need to download the latest versions.
- To download the plug-ins covered in this chapter, go to **http://www.softwarecenter.com**.

Acrobat Reader

- This is an extremely useful, if unspectacular, plug-in. If you work in publishing, or the printed media, you will have noticed that the page set-ups used on the Web are uncertain and there is little variation in the choice of fonts. On the other hand, Web pages are easy to display with all types of computer hardware.

- For those who want to see the same quality of page layout on the Web as on paper or want to use existing documents online without having to convert them, Adobe® created the Acrobat Reader. Documents supported by Acrobat Reader are in .pdf format.
- To read a .pdf document, click the link that leads to the document. Your browser will proceed to download Acrobat Reader, which opens in the browser window, and displays the document in question.
- Another solution (and a cheaper one, if you pay for dial-up access), is to download the document to your hard drive, then take the time to read it offline.

Below is the general procedure for downloading .pdf format documents from the Web.

- Point the mouse to the link that leads to the document.
- PC users: right-click the link.
  Mac users: press the Ctrl key down and click the link at the same time.
- In the menu that appears, choose the **Save Link As** (in Netscape Navigator) or **Save Target As** (in Internet Explorer) option.
- Choose where on your hard drive you want to save the document.
- Once you have disconnected, open Acrobat Reader, then the document you want to read.
- To download the Acrobat Reader plug-in, go to :
  http://www.adobe.co.uk.

Flash and Shockwave

- These are the most spectacular plug-ins. Created by Macromedia®, a specialist for Web and CDROM-application development tools, they will integrate your browser and turn it into a private theatre for the viewing of animations and special effects. However, you will need a computer that is reasonably recent to benefit. A list of sites that include demonstrations is available at the end of the book.

Media players: Real Player, QuickTime, Windows Media Player

- These plug-ins are, technically at least, still taking their first steps. The first time you see a video on the Web, you will certainly feel let down. When you see the postage stamp-sized image, inside an ugly, indiscreet frame, that jumps and flashes and is accompanied by a very odd soundtrack, who can blame you?
- You should not despair. Remember that images are difficult to send over the Internet, as is the soundtrack. A quality video requires not only a soundtrack, but also a minimum of 18 frames per second.
- If you wanted to watch a video on the Web that offers the same quality as your VCR, your connection would need to be able to handle 27 000 K per second. This is impossible, because even the best available connections can only provide 512 K per second (as you saw at the beginning of this book). So, in order for you to be able to receive a continuous video stream on your computer, the image and sound are "compressed with loss" so that they are the right size. Obviously, this results in a considerable loss of quality!
- These three plug-ins, which are incompatible, have been developed by three competitors: Realsystem®, Apple Corporation® and Microsoft®. Each company wants their system to dominate (naturally), but for the moment you will need all three to get the best from the Web.

If you are still unconvinced of the benefits of downloading from the Internet, have a look at what you can do with music.

MUSIC ON THE INTERNET

- The format known as MP3 has been responsible for a revolution in the music world. With MP3, you can benefit from a similar sound quality to a CD, but the file is ten times smaller!
- Now it is much easier to download music files, as the main obstacle - the file size - has been removed. With a high quality MP3 file, one minute of music uses 1 M.
- The biggest problem that remains with MP3 is not technical, but legal. Music, just like text and images, is protected by copyright. You will need to have the owner's permission before you can use it as you wish.
- Just because it is so easy to download from the Internet, it is not a reason to break the law. You should only download music that is not copyrighted, is offered free for promotional purposes, or music you have a CD copy of (or any other format that you have legally acquired). It goes without saying that selling tracks you have acquired illegally is itself illegal.
- You can, without breaking the law, download software that is capable of playing MP3 files. There is a wide choice of players, all of which are free, but the most popular is Winamp.

Download services

You may have been hesitant about joining the ranks of Internet users, perhaps because of worries about astronomical telephone bills, viruses, unsavoury Web sites - the list is long. It is true that the Internet has its negative aspects, but it can also provide you with the tools to protect yourself and your family.

SAFE WEB BROWSING

- An absolute must to protect your computer and all your data is **antivirus software**. You can obtain this, for free or for a charge, by downloading it. Even if you have bought software from a shop, you are strongly advised to update it regularly (every two weeks or so). You can update your software with all the latest virus remedies by using the tools provided with the software.
- If your children use the Internet, **parental control software**, which you should update regularly with downloads, will ensure they cannot access anything they should not see. This works using a list of sites, and each time the browser receives an address, the control software can authorise or block the page. You can, of course, choose the settings you require and add your own sites to the blacklist.

  For more information, see Part 6.
- In order to manage your Internet call costs, and to know how much time you spend online, install a **timer**.
- With **offline browsers** you can download an entire Web site, then take the time to read it while you are offline. This is a much better solution than saving a site manually, because to do that you have to visit each page individually, without missing any, and save it. An offline browser works automatically, and much faster than you can. Many also have the option of downloading several sites at once. You can also use this software to download temporary pages, or news stories, which will not always be available on the site.
- Advertisements are everywhere on the Web because they ensure an income for free Web services. You can use **advertisement suppression** software to limit the number of adverts you see.

You can make your life easier by using the numerous services available over the Internet, through the medium of downloads.

DOWNLOADABLE SERVICES

- The first companies to offer customer services over the Internet were, obviously, computer companies. They offer updates for software, drivers for various hardwares, online user manuals and so on.
- Today, all sorts of services are available to download, commercial or otherwise. You can download .pdf format (Acrobat Reader again) catalogues, product specifications, press releases, book reviews, order forms, application forms, instructions for all kinds of equipment, small programs called utilities, music extracts, video demonstrations, virtual visits of hotels, holiday resorts, houses... the list is endless.

If, like many Web surfers, you want to put your own personal pages online, talk about your hobbies, or share photographs with friends and family, downloading can provide the solutions you need.

DOWNLOADABLE TECHNICAL TOOLS

- You can download the tools necessary for **retouching your photos**, converting them to JPEG format (perfect for sharing them with friends, and essential if you want to display them on the Web), or optimising them (reducing the file size, therefore making them easier to send by e-mail or faster to download).
- **Graphics** tools are what you need to create graphics and small animations (gif animations).
- You can use **HTML editors** to create your own Web pages.
- Once you have prepared everything, you can put your work on the Web using **FTP software** (FTP = File Transfer Protocol). In this instance, you will be using the Internet to upload, because you are placing files on the Web, not retrieving them.
- See the "Finding specific software" section for information on how to find these tools.

Downloading files

You have found something that looks interesting, but you need to download it. No need to panic, there is nothing easier. The example below demonstrates how to download Acrobat Reader, the plug-in described previously.

DOWNLOADING THROUGH YOUR BROWSER

- If you are not already at a site from which you can download Acrobat Reader, go to **http://www.open.gov.uk** (this is just one example of a site which relies on the plug-in).
- In the list on the far right, click the **Adobe Acrobat Reader** logo.
- In the new page that appears, click the **Adobe Systems** link. When the Adobe® page opens in your browser, click the option to download **Acrobat Reader**.

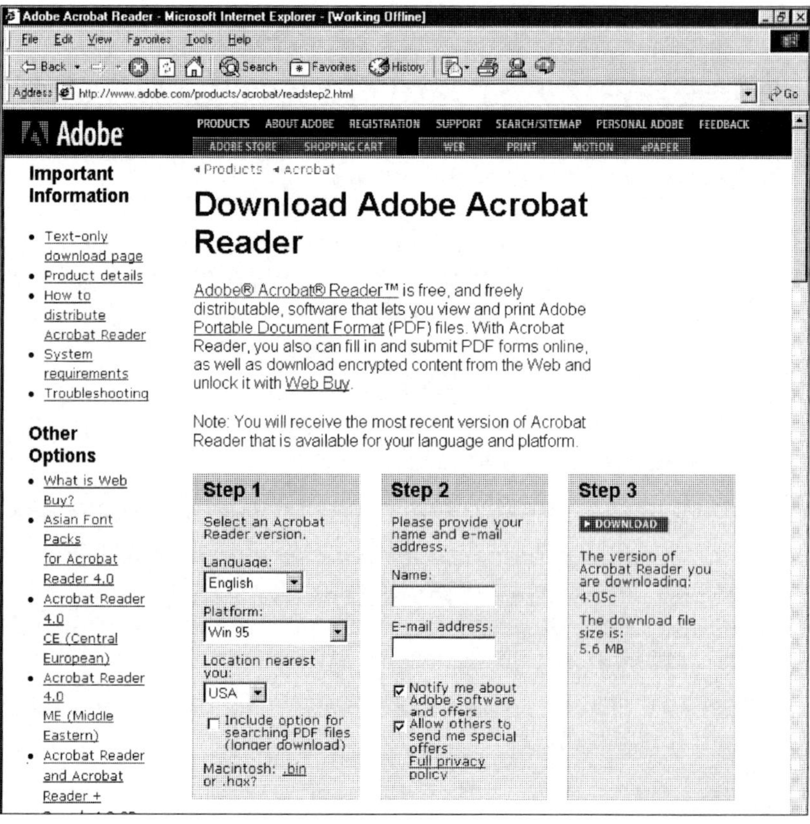

- Choose the appropriate options (**Language**, **Platform** and **Location nearest you**), and then click **DOWNLOAD** to receive the program.
- When the download finishes, double-click the file you have received to start the automatic installation.

If, after reading the previous pages, you have a sudden desire to download some of the software mentioned, the fastest way to find them is to go to a specialised download site (see also the list at the end of this book).

FINDING SPECIFIC SOFTWARE

- Some Web sites are entirely devoted to downloads. They include search engines and directories to help you find the exact software you want, by specifying your operating system (PC or Mac), and the sort of software you want. One such site can be found at **http://download.cnet.com/**

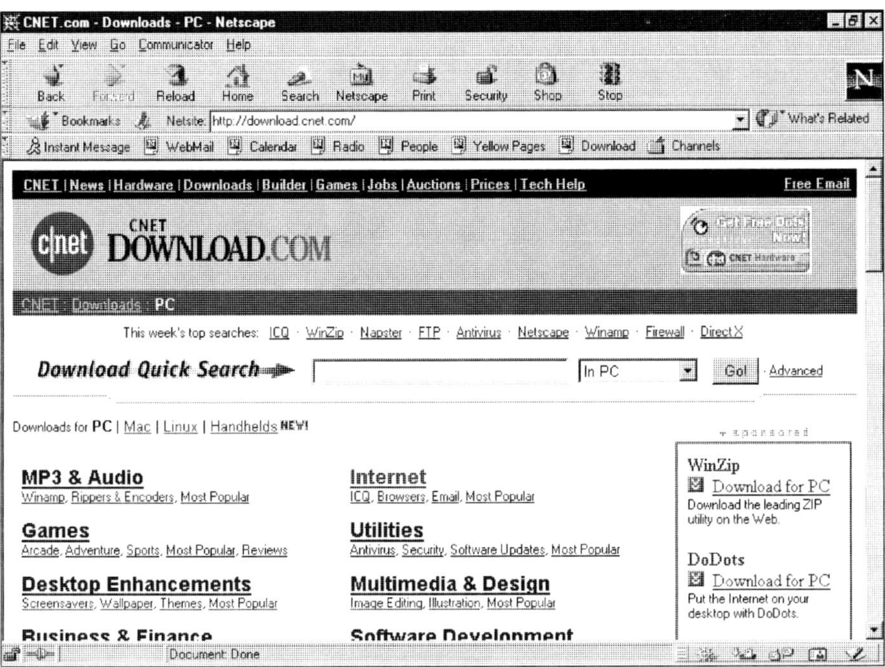

Downloading files

- You download software from either the editor's site or a dedicated FTP site.
- When you download from a Web site, the process is similar to that for Acrobat Reader.
- In the other case, you will arrive at a page like the one shown below, from which you should choose a site close to where you live in order to save time on the download. If the site you choose does not work, try another one.

Reliability	**Belgium**	Reliability	**Canada**
poor	ftp.linkline.be	poor	ftp.crc.doc.ca
poor	ftp.tornado.be	poor	ftp.direct.ca
Reliability	**Brazil**	Reliability	**Chile**
poor	ftp.iis.com.br	poor	sunsite.dcc.uchile.cl
poor	ftp.unicamp.br	Reliability	**China**
Reliability	**Czech Republic**	poor	ftp.pku.edu.cn
poor	ftp.eunet.cz	Reliability	**Bulgaria**
poor	ftp.zcu.cz	poor	ftp.eunet.bg
poor	pub.vse.cz		

A list of ftp sites from which you can download software.

Software, just like music, is the property of authors and publishers.

FREEWARE, SHAREWARE AND DEMOS

- You will find three categories of software on download sites: Freeware, Shareware and Demos. The category is always clearly indicated in the software description.

The software below is freeware. You do not have to pay anything and you can use the software as much as you like. Other freeware includes Aladdin Expander, Acrobat Reader and MP3 players:

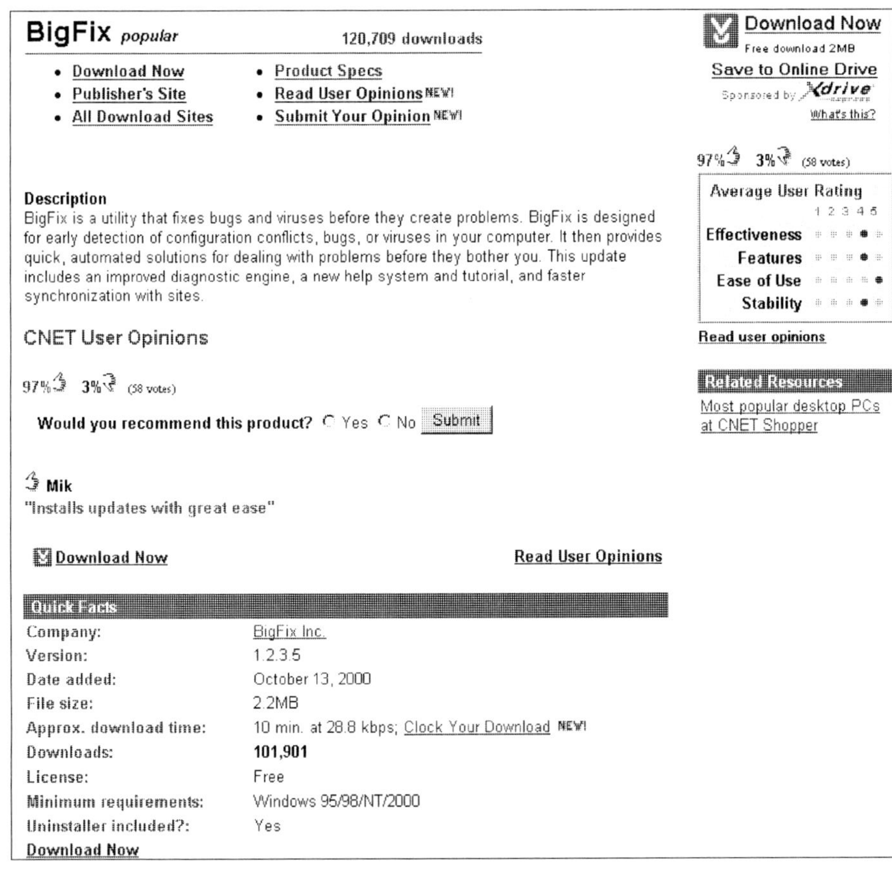
BigFix *popular* 120,709 downloads

- Download Now
- Publisher's Site
- All Download Sites
- Product Specs
- Read User Opinions NEW!
- Submit Your Opinion NEW!

Download Now
Free download 2MB
Save to Online Drive
Sponsored by Xdrive
What's this?

97% 3% (58 votes)

Average User Rating
1 2 3 4 5
Effectiveness
Features
Ease of Use
Stability
Read user opinions

Description
BigFix is a utility that fixes bugs and viruses before they create problems. BigFix is designed for early detection of configuration conflicts, bugs, or viruses in your computer. It then provides quick, automated solutions for dealing with problems before they bother you. This update includes an improved diagnostic engine, a new help system and tutorial, and faster synchronization with sites.

CNET User Opinions

97% 3% (58 votes)

Would you recommend this product? Yes No Submit

Mik
"Installs updates with great ease"

Download Now
Read User Opinions

Related Resources
Most popular desktop PCs at CNET Shopper

Quick Facts

Company:	BigFix Inc.
Version:	1.2.3.5
Date added:	October 13, 2000
File size:	2.2MB
Approx. download time:	10 min. at 28.8 kbps; Clock Your Download NEW!
Downloads:	**101,901**
License:	Free
Minimum requirements:	Windows 95/98/NT/2000
Uninstaller included?:	Yes

Download Now

Downloading files

- This is shareware. You can use this software to try it out, but if you decide to keep it, you will need to pay the editor:

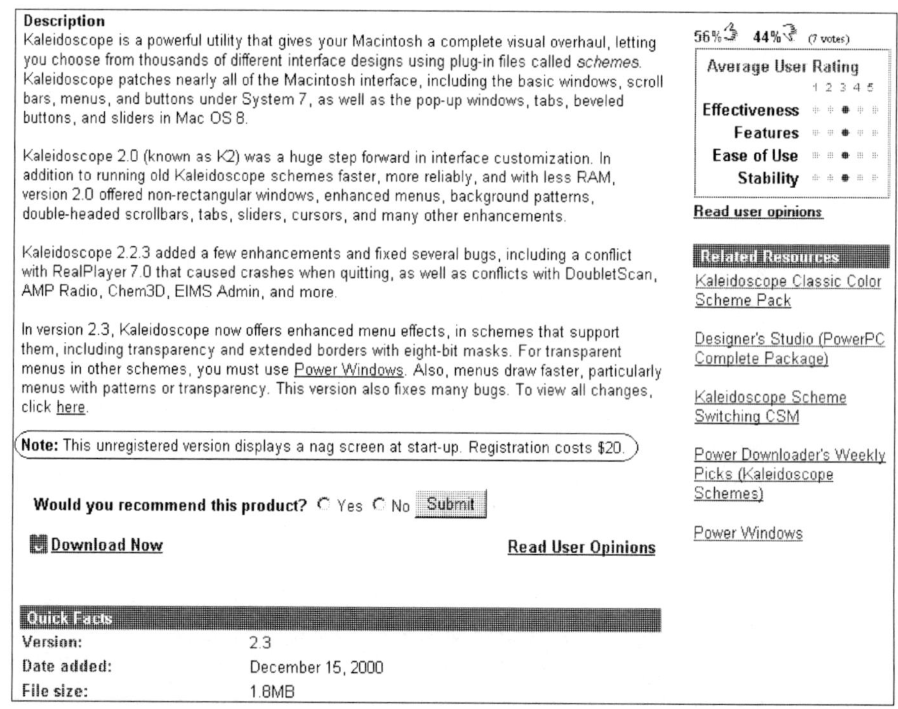

Description
Kaleidoscope is a powerful utility that gives your Macintosh a complete visual overhaul, letting you choose from thousands of different interface designs using plug-in files called *schemes*. Kaleidoscope patches nearly all of the Macintosh interface, including the basic windows, scroll bars, menus, and buttons under System 7, as well as the pop-up windows, tabs, beveled buttons, and sliders in Mac OS 8.

Kaleidoscope 2.0 (known as K2) was a huge step forward in interface customization. In addition to running old Kaleidoscope schemes faster, more reliably, and with less RAM, version 2.0 offered non-rectangular windows, enhanced menus, background patterns, double-headed scrollbars, tabs, sliders, cursors, and many other enhancements.

Kaleidoscope 2.2.3 added a few enhancements and fixed several bugs, including a conflict with RealPlayer 7.0 that caused crashes when quitting, as well as conflicts with DoubletScan, AMP Radio, Chem3D, EIMS Admin, and more.

In version 2.3, Kaleidoscope now offers enhanced menu effects, in schemes that support them, including transparency and extended borders with eight-bit masks. For transparent menus in other schemes, you must use Power Windows. Also, menus draw faster, particularly menus with patterns or transparency. This version also fixes many bugs. To view all changes, click here.

Note: This unregistered version displays a nag screen at start-up. Registration costs $20.

Would you recommend this product? Yes No Submit

Download Now

Read User Opinions

Quick Facts

Version:	2.3
Date added:	December 15, 2000
File size:	1.8MB

56% 44% (7 votes)

Average User Rating

	1 2 3 4 5
Effectiveness	
Features	
Ease of Use	
Stability	

Read user opinions

Related Resources

Kaleidoscope Classic Color Scheme Pack

Designer's Studio (PowerPC Complete Package)

Kaleidoscope Scheme Switching CSM

Power Downloader's Weekly Picks (Kaleidoscope Schemes)

Power Windows

- Shareware is very often a small program designed for simple and precise tasks. When you download shareware, the version may be incomplete, or you may only be able to use it for a limited time. If you do not like the shareware, simply remove it from your computer.

- Demos are commercial software whose functions have been limited to a given time span or restricted, so that potential buyers can try them:

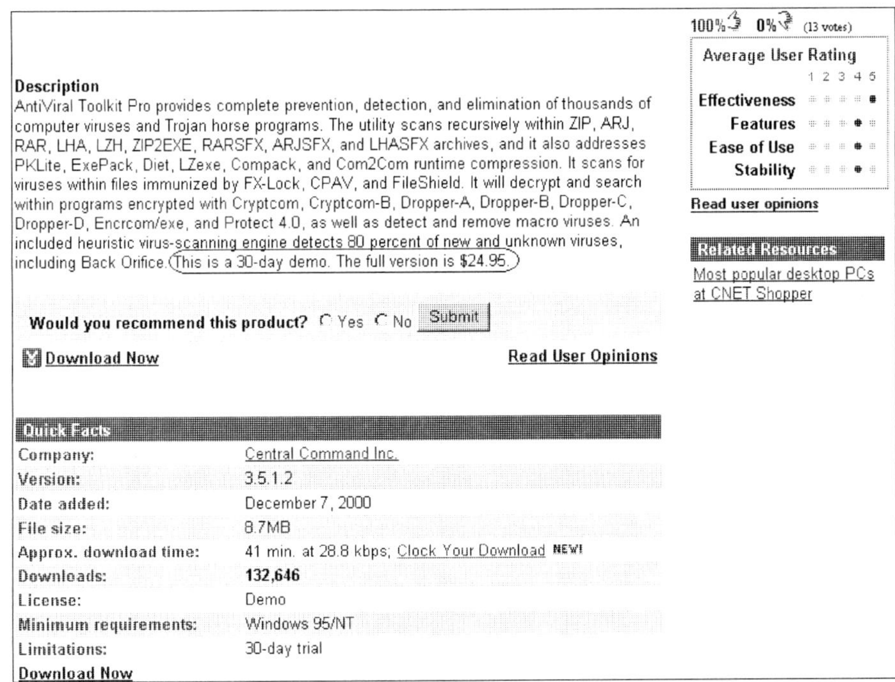

If you have found a real jewel, but the file is large and your connection cuts off five minutes before the download is complete, there is no need to panic. There is a solution!

USING A DOWNLOAD UTILITY

- The Internet is not flawless and often network problems mean that a download is interrupted.

  For small files, this is not a problem, as you can just reconnect and start again.

- However, downloading large files over a telephone line can take one, two or more hours. If this is the case, try using a download utility such as **Go!Zilla** or **Getright**, which allows you to restart an interrupted download where you left off.

Compressed files

An oversized file is a cumbersome thing. Fortunately there is an easy way to slim your files down...!

WHY COMPRESS FILES?

- You have already learned about the torturous compression applied to video files. However, you can also compress files without doing them any harm and then transport them simply and quickly.
- The type of compression described in this section should be used in the following, typical, cases:
  - sending a large (anything over 1 M) attachment by e-mail,
  - sending several files as e-mail attachments,
  - distributing freeware, which is often composed of several files,
  - saving time when downloading and uploading.

It will not be long before you come across some of these oddly named files.

PC AND MAC COMPRESSION FORMATS

- When a filename is followed by a full stop and one of these extensions, it is a compressed file:
  - .arc, .arj, .pak, .hqx, .gz, .z,
  - .bin, .mim, .mime, .b64, .pf,
  - .sit, .sea,
  - .uu, .uue, .zip.
- In the **PC** world, the most common compression format is Zip. Compressed files are called **filename.zip**.
  All you need to do is decompress these files, or unzip them. The common terms are zipping and unzipping.
- For **Mac** users, there are two popular compression formats:
  - BinHex: compressed files are called **filename.hqx**,
  - MacBinary: look for files called **filename.bin**.

These compressed files will first need to be decompressed **then** decoded before they return to their normal form. The decompression tool first creates an intermediary file called **filename.sit**, which is decompressed but still encoded, then it decodes the file.

Why not try a simple and practical decompression tool?

USING THE ALADDIN EXPANDER DECOMPRESSION UTILITY

- First you need to download the Aladdin Expander utility (in the right version for your computer) from a download site, or from http://www.aladdinsys.com. Install the program and start it.
- Move your windows around so that the little Aladdin Expander window and the window that contains the file you want to decompress are side by side.
- Drag the file in question into the Aladdin Expander window.

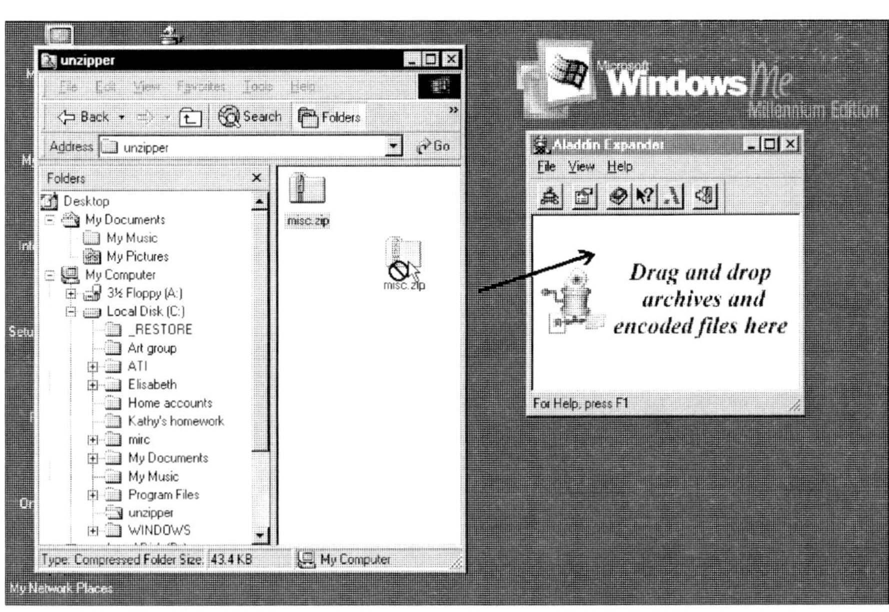

As soon as you release the mouse button, the utility starts to work:

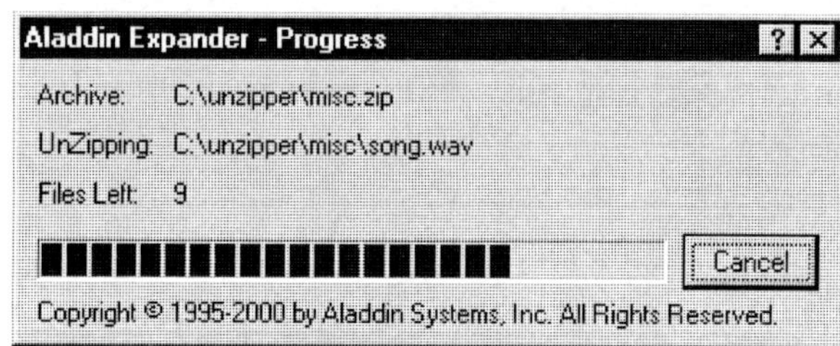

Once the decompression is finished, all the decompressed files are neatly stored in a new folder that has the same name as the original file.

- Open this folder to see the files inside:

If you are convinced that compressing files is useful, now you will want to really get started.

COMPRESSING FILES

- If you compress desktop software files, you will be surprised at the space you save. However, sound, image and video files are already highly optimised, so compression will only save about 20% more disk space. Still, it is the best solution if you want to group several files into one, but watch out for the total size.
- If you work on a **PC**, you can use WinZip, a utility that will compress and decompress, or DropStuff, which is Aladdin Expander's "little brother" and is just as practical. WinZip is very common on PC, but a bit difficult to master.
- **Mac** users should use DropStuff (better known as Stuffit Expander).

WinZip and DropStuff are shareware, so you need to buy them at the end of the trial period.

Everyone is talking about the Internet. It is in all the media and is often a subject of controversy. This section will help you to form your own opinion about the technology. Of coursethe Internet itself is full of Web pages, discussion forums etc, where you can find out about and debate Internet topics.

6th Part

More information

Security

With three hundred million users across the world, there have to be some bad apples amongst them.

PROTECTING YOUR COMPUTER

- Some hackers are computer geniuses, they attack big targets. Others, however, make use of the widely available Internet tools to attack, completely at random, private users.
- PCs that run Windows are most at risk, simply because it is the most common and well-known operating system.
- Here are a few simple rules you should keep to:
  - make regular downloads to update Windows or Mac OS (from the editor's site), and update your desktop and e-mail programs at the same time.
  - install an antivirus utility and keep it up to date. Choose only one antivirus, otherwise you could have conflict problems.
  - if you have a permanent Internet connection (by cable or ADSL, for example), you should use a firewall.
  - when you configure your browser, leave the default security options.

Defining Internet Explorer's security settings

- **Tools - Internet Options - Security** tab
- Click the **Internet** icon then **Custom Level** button.
- Make sure the **ActiveX controls and plug-ins** option is **Enable**.

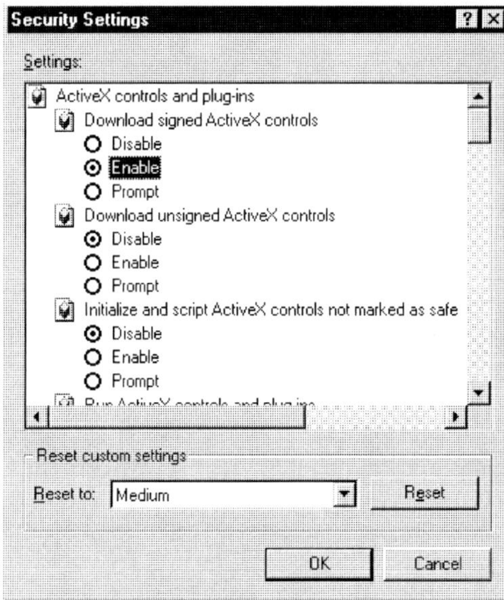

▒ **Tools** - **Internet Options** - **Advanced** tab

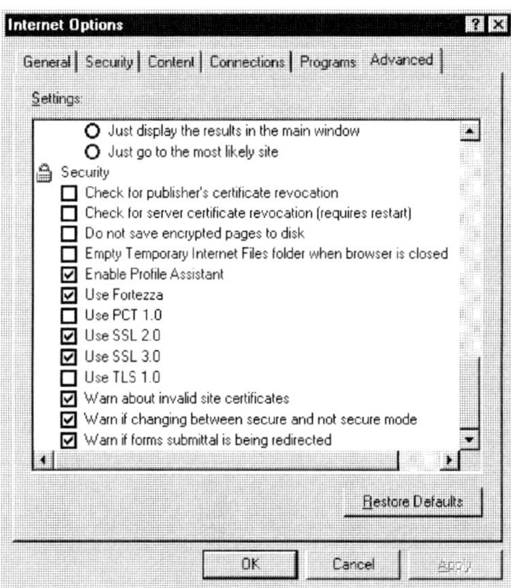

▒ Click the **Restore Defaults** button to activate the essential options.

Security

Often, the weak link in your protection is your password. Make sure that it is not too easy to guess.

CHOOSING A GOOD PASSWORD

- Passwords enable you to protect your computer, your files, and personal information you might give over the Internet.
- In the future, you will need to use a password dozens of times every day for simple operations (getting into your house, withdrawing money, switching on the oven remotely and so on). It makes sense to know how to create them!
- What not to do:
  - use the names of your friends and family, birth dates, or common nouns.
  - accept a password that is assigned to you. For example, change the password your ISP gave you, if you can.
  - allow a system to remember your password for you.
- Tips for good passwords:
  - use about eight characters,
  - use the first letters of a sentence,
  - try two short words, joined by a number or hyphen. e.g. **pass2word** or **pass-word**,
  - write phonetically instead of using accepted spelling: faunettikly,
  - use a combination of upper and lower case letters and use special characters if you can,
  - try a mathematical, chemical or physical equation or formula (but not $e=mc^2$, too obvious!),
  - combine this advice.

Cookies: friend or foe? Before you decide, discover what they are.

COOKIES

Definition

- A cookie is a short character string that is placed in a file on your computer by your browser when you visit Web sites. This site, and only this site, can retrieve the string at any time. There are two kinds of cookie:
  - **temporary cookies** remain on your computer for no longer than the time you are connected to the Internet and they are deleted when you close your browser.
  - **permanent cookies** are stored as files on your computer and remain there even after you close your browser.
- Here is some of the information they contain:
  - the date and time you visited the site,
  - the answers to a questionnaire you might have completed at the site,
  - personal information retrieved by the server.

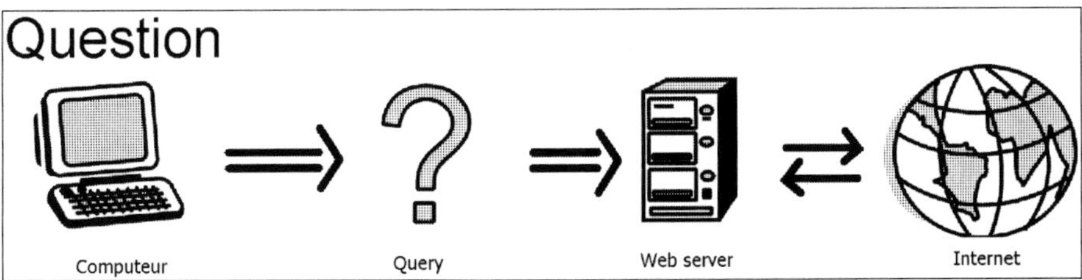

The browser seeks a Web page using a Web address.
To do this, it sends a query to a Web server.

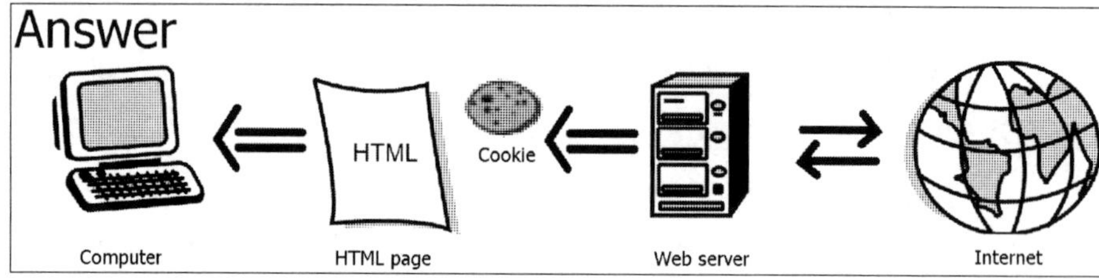

When the server answers the query, it sends a Web page which is accompanied by an instruction to create a cookie. The brower will do this on your hard drive.

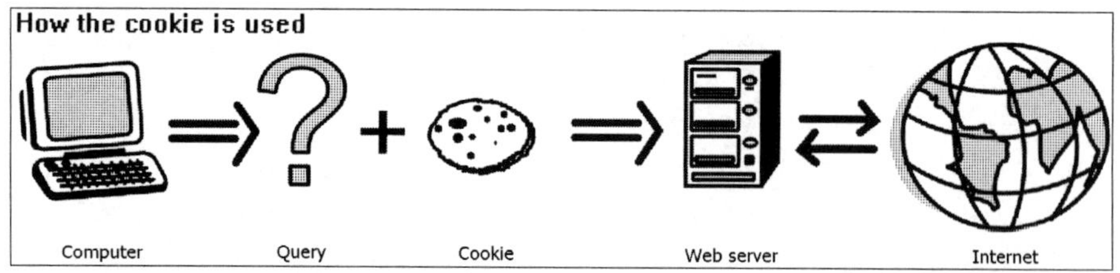

For each Web page query, the brower will check if it can find a cookie that corresponds to the address. If it finds one, it will send the cookie to the Web server along with the query. The server can process the cookie in a number of ways, such as sending a particular page, or compiling statistics.

Changing the permissions for cookies in Internet Explorer

Internet Explorer 5.0 authorises the creation of cookies on your computer by default. You can change this setting.

- **Tools** - **Internet Options** - **Security** tab
- Click the **Internet** icon then the **Custom Level** button.
- Scroll down the categories until you reach **Cookies**.

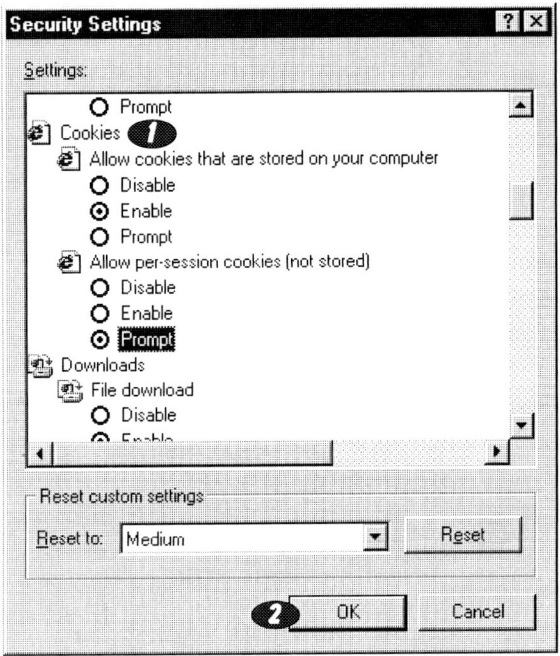

1. For each cookie type (**Allow cookies that are stored on your computer** for permanent cookies and **Allow per-session cookies (not stored)** for temporary cookies), activate one of the following choices:

   Disable Internet Explorer will refuse cookies.

   Enable Internet Explorer will accept cookies without asking you.

   Prompt Internet Explorer will ask you before accepting cookies.

2. Click **OK** to confirm your changes.

Viewing/deleting cookies with Internet Explorer 5

By default, Internet Explorer stores cookies in the following folders: C:\Windows\Cookies and C:\Windows\Temporary Internet Files.

- To see the Cookies folder, open the **Windows Explorer** using **Start - Programs - Windows Explorer**.
- In the left-hand pane, select the **Windows** file, then double-click the **Cookies** folder in the right-hand pane.

  A list of cookies appears in the right-hand pane.
- To delete cookies from the Windows\Cookies folder, select them and press Del.
- Confirm the deletion by clicking **OK**.

  While you may have deleted cookies from the Windows\Cookies folder, they are still present in C:\Windows\Temporary Internet Files.
- To delete cookies from Windows\Temporary Internet Files, use **Tools - Internet Options**. In the **General** tab, click the **Settings** button in the **Temporary internet files** frame.
- Click the **View Files** button.

  The contents of the C:\Windows\Temporary Internet Files folder appear in a new window.
- Click the **Type** column header to sort the folder by file type.

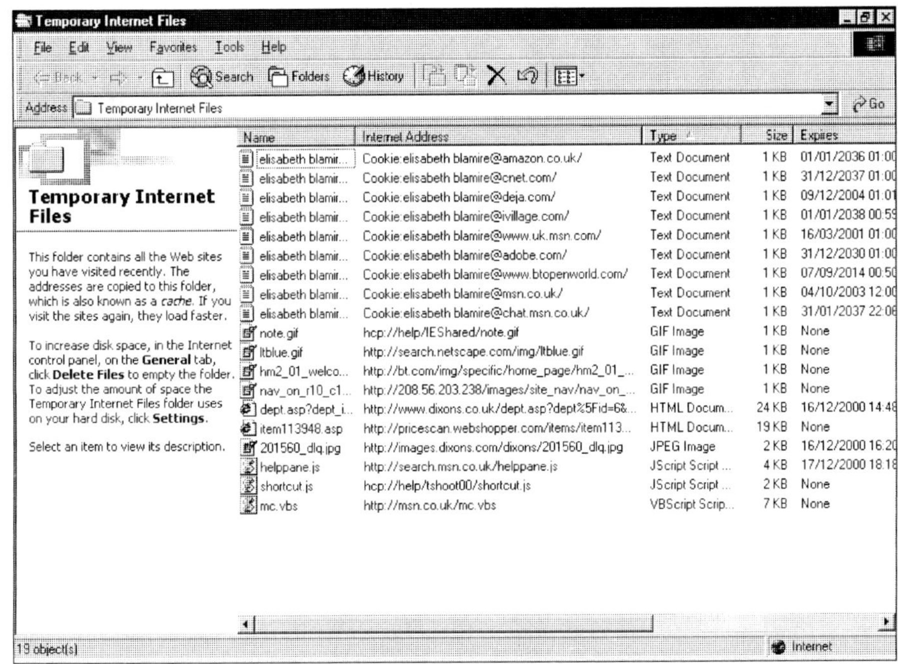

*Cookies are **Text Document** files and their name begins with the username.*

- Select them, then press Del.

Changing the permissions for cookies in Netscape Navigator

- **Edit - Preferences**
- Click the **Advanced** category.

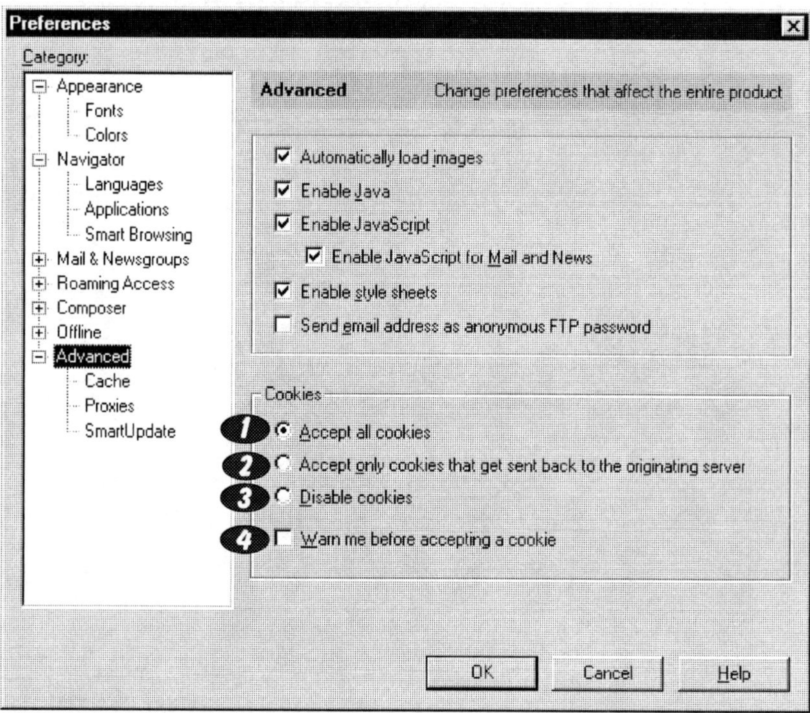

1. All cookies sent by sites will be created on your computer.
2. Only temporary cookies will be accepted.
3. All cookies with be rejected, in which case, you may not be able to access some sites.
4. Activate this option if you want to be asked each time whether or not to accept a cookie.

Viewing/deleting cookies with Netscape Navigator

- By default, Netscape stores cookies in a file in the Netscape folder:
  - On a PC: C:\Windows\Program Files\Netscape\Users\default\cookies.txt
  - On a Mac: use the Sherlock utility to search for the word "cookies".
- Open the file in WordPad (PC) or SimpleText (Mac) to view the cookies.
- To delete all or some of the cookies, delete the file contents and save it using **File - Save**.

E-commerce sites are aware of the dangers of buying over the Internet and have put in place systems that are designed to protect customers.

BUYING OVER THE INTERNET

- E-commerce sites are secure.
- An encoded site is equipped for the transfer of confidential information (such as your credit card number) without any risk of interference. When you visit a secure site, your browser alerts you with a message like this one:

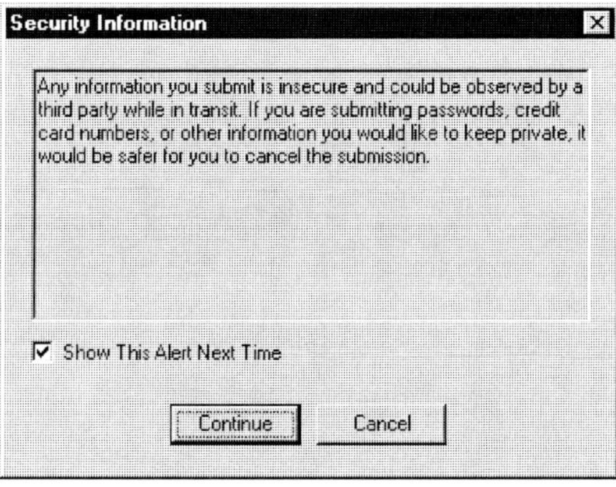

- Click **Continue**.

Security

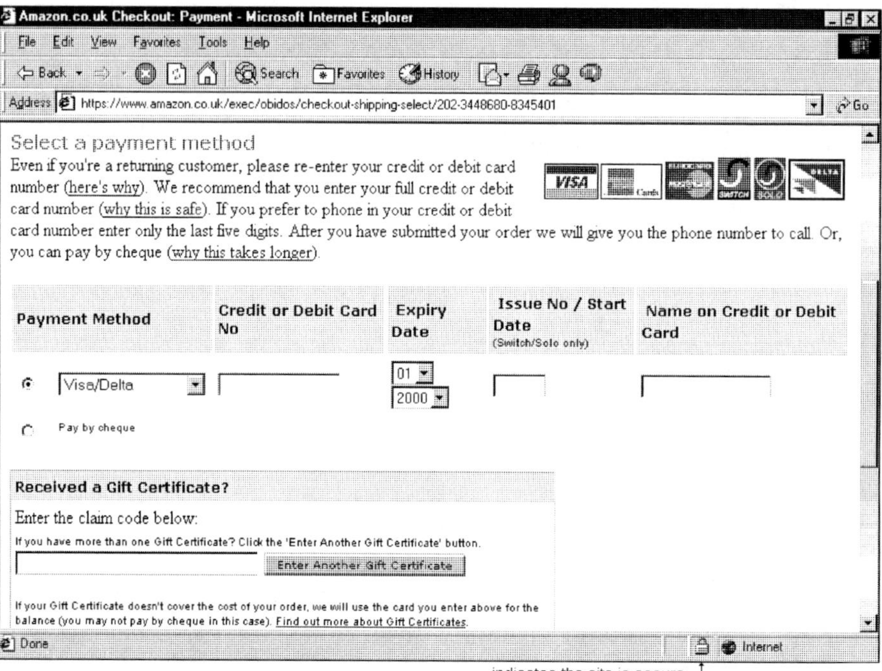

indicates the site is secure

- To check a page's security information:
  - in Internet Explorer, use **File - Properties** and click the **Certificates** button, or click the 🔒 icon on the status bar.
  - in Netscape Navigator: **Communicator - Tools - Security Information**, or the Security button, or double-click the 🔒 icon on the status bar, or Ctrl Shift **I**.

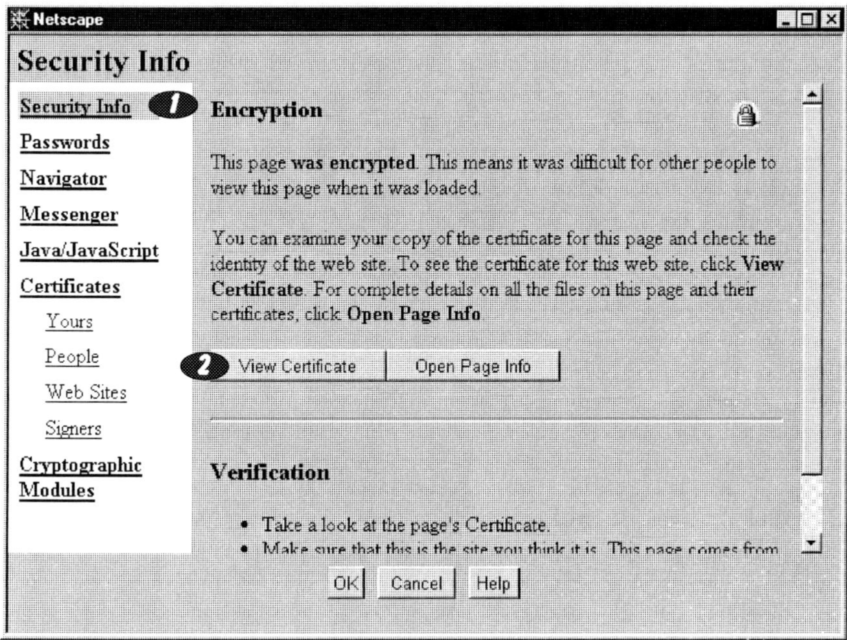

1. If necessary, activate this category.
2. Click here to see the site's certificate.

- E-commerce sites explain their security systems and offer guarantees to consumers. For example, below is **Amazon.co.uk**'s security policy:

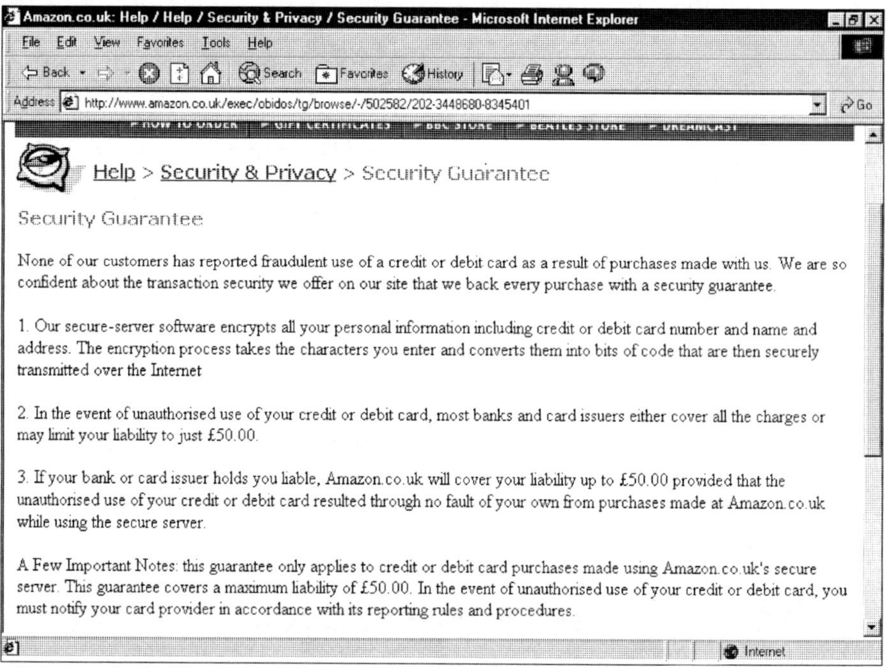

Amazon.co.uk: Help / Help / Security & Privacy / Security Guarantee - Microsoft Internet Explorer

Address http://www.amazon.co.uk/exec/obidos/tg/browse/-/502582/202-3448680-8345401

Help > Security & Privacy > Security Guarantee

Security Guarantee

None of our customers has reported fraudulent use of a credit or debit card as a result of purchases made with us. We are so confident about the transaction security we offer on our site that we back every purchase with a security guarantee.

1. Our secure-server software encrypts all your personal information including credit or debit card number and name and address. The encryption process takes the characters you enter and converts them into bits of code that are then securely transmitted over the Internet

2. In the event of unauthorised use of your credit or debit card, most banks and card issuers either cover all the charges or may limit your liability to just £50.00.

3. If your bank or card issuer holds you liable, Amazon.co.uk will cover your liability up to £50.00 provided that the unauthorised use of your credit or debit card resulted through no fault of your own from purchases made at Amazon.co.uk while using the secure server.

A Few Important Notes: this guarantee only applies to credit or debit card purchases made using Amazon.co.uk's secure server. This guarantee covers a maximum liability of £50.00. In the event of unauthorised use of your credit or debit card, you must notify your card provider in accordance with its reporting rules and procedures.

- Here are some common sense tips on how to avoid Internet fraud:
  - Take the time to evaluate the e-commerce site you are visiting. Does the company have a physical address and telephone number specified on the site?
  - Read the conditions of sale and, importantly, the exchange and refund conditions. What are your rights?
  - Be extra careful when you are buying from a site situated abroad. Technical specifications differ greatly (such as power cables, DVD zones, colour encoding for VHS cassettes and so forth). Postage and packing costs could be considerable, and you may be liable for sales taxes, duty payments and your credit card company may make a charge for a foreign currency payment. Furthermore, if you have a complaint, the law of the country of purchase applies.

If your children are avid surfers...

PARENTAL CONTROL

- Parental control software, such as Cyper Patrol, CyberSitter and Net Nanny, is available to buy or download (shareware, freeware and demos). They are updated every time you go online, ensuring that their blacklist of forbidden sites is always up to date. If one of these sites is requested by the browser, whether it be intentional or not, the parental control software refuses access to the site. You can change the settings to suit your needs and add any sites you consider unsuitable (such as sites with a sexual content, foul language, violence, racism, Internet hacking, firearms etc...).
- Some ISPs, such as AOL, who charge for their services offer a good quality parental control service.
- Browsers themselves have a suppression facility, but they have a huge drawback - their blacklist is based on voluntary inscription by the sites themselves!

Who runs the Internet?

Here are a few basic facts about the Internet.

INTERNET HISTORY

- The Internet has military origins: how can you be sure of failsafe, secure communications between computers, even in wartime?
- In the early 1960s, a section of the US Defense Department, called the ARPA, created the ARPANet network, whose goal was to ensure the communication between all types of computers and the transfer of data between them.
- The key to this network was the decentralisation of data transfer. The principle was that, as soon as one communication line is cut, the computers would simply search for another path to transfer data.
- Suppose that two towns are linked by one single cable. If this cable is destroyed, the towns can no longer communicate. To get around this problem, a town needs to be linked to several towns. Now, if a cable is destroyed, the town can still communicate by passing via another town.

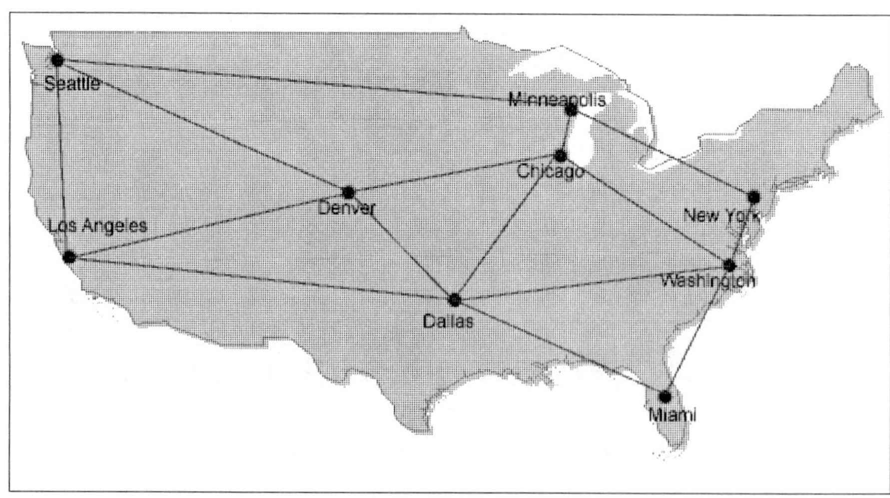

More information

- In 1972, after an international conference on the possibility of linking all computers and networks together, a working group was given the task of finding a protocol that could provide such a connection. The result of their work was the creation of the TCP/IP protocol.
- At the beginning of the 80s, after several networks (universities and military installations) had been linked together, ARPANet became the INTERNET (INTERnational NETwork).
- The Internet began to expand to universities, research laboratories, big companies etc...
- Some medium-sized companies and enthusiastic private users decided to get together to create private services. This is where private Internet access providers came from. They were known as "Providers".
- In 1992, the Web appeared, along with user-friendly tools and the network began to grow at a phenomenal rate.

While nobody is actually in charge of the Internet, there are organisations that, amongst other things, define standards, distribute IP addresses and develop new protocols.

THE INTERNATIONAL ORGANISATIONS

- When the Internet was created, the task of developing protocols was assigned to the Internet Configuration Control Board. In 1983, this former committee, now an independent association (Internet Activities Board, or **IAB**), was given the job of defining new communication standards for inter-system communication and at the same time conserving the basic network protocols.
- The **IAB** created the Internet Engineering Task Force (**IETF**), whose job it is, amongst other things, to solve any problems that arise on the network, such as technical norms, the standardisation of tools proposed by commercial entities and the overloading of principle "routes". As the IETF is organised as an association, volunteers are needed to participate in the working groups that are created whenever there is a major problem to be solved.
- The **IAB** also created the Internet Research Task Force (**IRTF**), which carries out long-term research on the network's future.

- Next, the **IESG** and **IRSG** committees were created to act as parent bodies to the different groups of the IETF and the IRTF, because the IAB was not enough.
- In 1992, the **IAB** became the Internet's standard bearer. It was renamed as the Internet Architecture Board and given the mission of supervising all the committees to ensure that their work is coherent.
- At the same time, all the organisations related to the Internet came together to form a non-profit-making organisation: the Internet Society (**ISOC**), which is charged with discussing the network's future development.
- The United Kingdom has two local ISOC chapters, ISOC England and ISOC Scotland. They both have the aim of promoting Internet use in their respective countries and allow the main Internet actors and users to come together to exchange ideas about the Internet and its use and evolution.
- Another important organisation is the World Wide Web Consortium: **W3C**. This group takes charge of the technical development of the Web by introducing common standards for the needs of the Web, such as the HTML language.

.com, .co.uk, .org - find it all confusing?

DOMAIN NAMES

- There are two main domain name families:
  - **International domain names** such as .com, .net and .org. These are distributed on the basis of "first come, first served", no matter where in the world the site is based. For example edinburgh-news.com is the Edinburgh Evening News local newspaper, and nike.com is self-explanatory.
  - **Geographical domain names**: each country has its "flag" in cyberspace and uses it as it feels appropriate.
- The rules for geographical domain names are defined by a national organisation in each country and can be consulted online. For the UK, go to: **http://www.nic.uk**.

- The Internet also has "flags of convenience". Some small countries have flexible naming rules in order to attract sites to their geographical domain name. In the United States, geographical names are defined by state. For example, Texans can use tx.com.
- The attribution of international domain names was controlled by an American government organisation for quite some time. This arrangement, unique in the Internet and contrary to its principles, was hotly contested.

  Now, domain names are assigned by the ICANN (International Corporation for Assigned Names and Numbers), which is based in California. The ICANN has accredited regional registrars in order to limit any centralist tendencies.
- Below is a list of the accredited registrars in the UK:
  - **http://www.easyspace.com**,
  - **http://www.totalregistrations.com**,
  - **http://www.vi.net**,
  - **http://www.nominate.net**.

Future developments

If you have become convinced of the benefits and uses of the services available on the Internet, you are not alone.

TOMORROW'S INTERNET

- Internet has become a victim of its own success:
  - overloading and slow access over ordinary telephone lines,
  - the difficulty of mastering computers: they are quite expensive and some find them complicated,
  - developing countries are a long way behind, mainly because of inadequate telephone infrastructures: 50% of adults have never used a telephone.
- Engineers and telecoms specialists are not dithering, and they are already putting tomorrow's solutions in place. This section will take a closer look at these avenues.
- Technical developments are evolving all the time. Keep up to date with these sites:
  - **http://www.guardianunlimited.co.uk/online**: the Online supplement from The Guardian newspaper,
  - **http://www.internetnews.com**: all the latest news from the Internet business world,
  - **http://www.independent.co.uk/news/Digital**: the Independent's technology supplement.

You can use the Internet without knowing how to use a computer...

INTERNET ON THE TELEVISION

- A recent development has been clever boxes that enable you to access Internet via your television. Some say that it is an incomplete Internet, because the only available services are the Web and e-mail.
- Televisions do not have a hard drive, so you cannot profit from downloading services, plug-ins, nor newsgroup and forum services.

- Another drawback with the current systems is the transmission of data using a remote control, which is fiddly, or a keyboard, which is cumbersome. Voice recognition, which is still very much a gadget today, could be an ideal solution.

Internet all the time, wherever you are?

THE MOBILE INTERNET

On mobile telephones

- The magic word here is **WAP** (Wireless Application Protocol): a new Internet protocol for wireless communications.
- WAP-enabled telephones, the latest generation, give you access to a mini-Internet, over a low-capacity link (9.6 K/per second), on a small screen.
- Check out WAP at **http://www.gelon.net** to get a better idea of what it is all about.

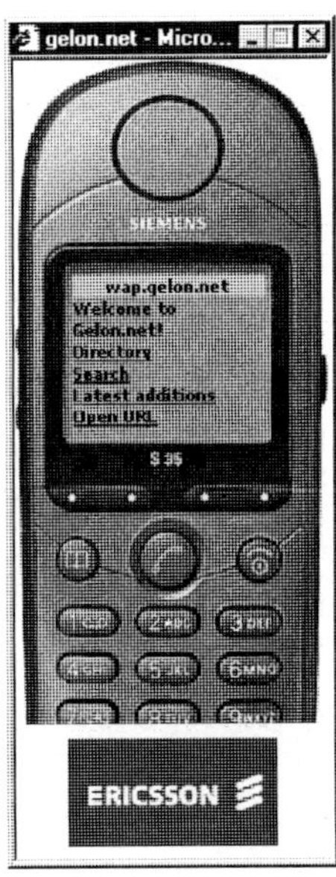

Future developments

- Web sites need to be re-written so that they are compatible with WAP.

On PDAs (Personal Digital Assistants)

- These pocket assistants include a diary, address book and mini versions of the main desktop applications. Now they are getting ready for the Internet.
- New-generation PDAs, which are equipped with tiny modems and colour screens, can connect to the Internet via a standard telephone jack.
- Here too, Web sites will need to be adapted and simplified. Browsers that have been developed especially for this sort of use can already simplify pages automatically, in which case text is generally the only element that remains.

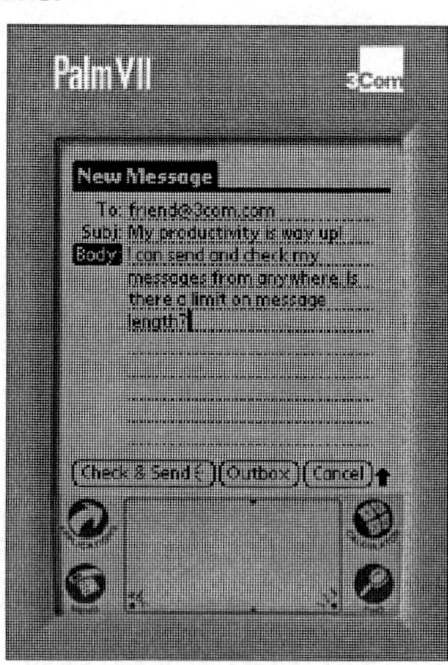

E-mail works and even supports attached files!

- You can access forums and chat using Yahoo! Messenger, after downloading the appropriate software.

Electricity? Really?

INTERNET THROUGH ELECTRICAL WIRES

- The leader in this domain is a Swiss company called ASCOM, which is currently carrying out large-scale tests in Germany. The technology in question is called **PLC** (Power Line Communication) and soon (perhaps in 2002) you will be able to buy an adapter that can turn your electrical sockets into Internet access points.
- The system uses a high frequency broadband transmission with a very low wattage (10mW), to avoid interference with household electrical appliances.
- The connection speed is 7 M/per second.
- If this application proves to be commercially viable, it could be tomorrow's solution. In rural areas of developed countries, it will be a better option than ADSL; in the developing world, hundreds of households could connect to the Internet. For example, only 24% of Brazilian homes have a telephone, but 95% have electricity.

List of sites

Themed directories

http://www.yahoo.co.uk

http://www.excite.co.uk

http://www.godado.co.uk

http://www.mckinley.com

Index-based search engines

http://www.google.com

http://www.hotbot.com

http://www.altavista.co.uk

Mixed search tools

http://www.looksmart.co.uk

http://www.infoseek.co.uk

http://www.ukplus.co.uk

http://www.ask.com

Other tools

http://www.beaucoup.com - a complete directory of search engines

http://www.strategic-road.com - strategic links, specialist directories and search engines in French and English

Download sites

http://www.download.com

http://www.shareware.com

http://www.tucows.com

Directories and street maps

http://www.mappy.com
http://www.uk.yell.com

Internet guides

http://www.learnthenet.com
http://www.internet.com
http://www.ukonline.com
http://www.whatsnew.com - new sites
http://www.stpt.com - recommended sites

Service providers

http://www.nic.uk
http://www.ukfreeisps.abelgratis.co.uk - a guide to free ISPs in the UK

Online trading

http://www.etrade.co.uk
http://www.londonstockexchange.com/

Press and media

http://news.bbc.co.uk
http://www.guardianunlimited.co.uk/online
http://www.independent.co.uk
http://www.dailymail.co.uk
http://www.dailytelegraph.co.uk

List of sites

Cinema

http://www.oscars.com

http://www.insideout.co.uk - complete listings for all UK cinemas

http://www.bfi.org.uk - British Film Institute official site

http://www.nftsfilm-tv.ac.uk

http://humblepenguin.tripod.com

http://members.tripod.com/umq/umq.htm - a variety of movie quotes

http://www.britishpictures.com

http://www.hazelgrove4.demon.co.uk

Music

http://www.nme.com

http://www.mtv.com

http://www.dotmusic.com

http://www.digibox.com

http://www.previewtunes.com

http://www.audioweb.co.uk

Record labels

http://www.universalmusic.com

http://www.sonymusic.com

http://www.bluenote.com

Festivals

http://www.reading-festival.com

http://www.edfringe.com - Edinburgh Festival Fringe

http://www.glastonbury-festival.com

http://www.lff.org.uk - London Film Festival official site

http://www.bigfestivals.com - directory of UK music festivals

http://www.eif.co.uk - Edinburgh International Festival official site

http://www.festivals.demon.co.uk

MP3 music

http://www.mp3.com

http://www.listen.com

http://www.audiofind.com

http://www.mp3now.com

Books

http://www.amazon.co.uk

http://www.waterstones.co.uk

http://www.bol.com

http://www.bl.uk - The British Library

http://www.ebooknet.com

http://www.nls.ac.uk - The National Library of Scotland

http://www.booksatoz.com

http://www.editions-eni.com

Photography

http://www.photgraphyreview.com

http://www.azuswebworks.com/photography/index.html

http://www.nmpft.org.uk

Theatre and dance

http://britishtheatre.miningco.com

http://www.on-broadway.com/links

http://www.musicalscollection.com

List of sites

http://www.dancemuseum.org

http://www.bridgewater-hall.co.uk

http://www.dellarte.com

http://www.shakespeares-globe.org

http://www.eft.co.uk - The Edinburgh Festival Theatre

http://www.rsc.org.uk - The Royal Shakespeare Company

http://www.royalopera.org

Museums

http://www.bronte.org.uk

http://www.nmpft.org.uk

http://www.dancemuseum.org

http://www.thebritishmuseum.ac.uk

http://www.npg.org.uk - The National Portrait Gallery

http://www.nms.ac.uk - The National Museum of Scotland

http://www.nhm.ac.uk - The Natural History Museum

http://www.lakelandmuseum.org.uk

http://www.newlanark.org - The New Lanark World Heritage Site

Sport

http://www.sportsonline.co.uk

http://sport.bbc.co.uk

http://british-athletics.co.uk

http://www.irishsportscouncil.ie

http://www.alpchallenge.com

http://www.tourdestrees.org

http://www.wimbledon.org

http://www.commonwealthgames2002.org.uk

http://www.americascup.org

http://www.ecb.co.uk

http://www.standrewsopen.com

http://www.btcc.co.uk

http://www.rugbyleagueonline.freeserve.co.uk

http://www.24h-le-mans.com

http://www.euroskating2000.com

http://www.2001.edmonton.com

http://www.6nations.co.uk

http://www.slc2002.org

http://www.cricketunlimited.co.uk

http://www.silverstone-circuit.co.uk

Travel

http://www.countryconnect.co.uk

http://www.aroundtheworlds.com

http://www.lonelyplanet.com

http://www.travel.roughguides.com

http://www.wherenext.com

http://www.fodors.com

Flash animations

http://www.thematrix.co.uk

http://www.discovery.com/highspeed/tlc/mummies

http://www.jacobscreek.com.au

http://www.tedbaker.co.uk

Glossary

ADSL (Asymmetric Digital Subscriber Line)

A technology that uses high frequencies in standard telephone lines in order to transmit data (such as e-mail and Web pages), leaving the lower frequency bandwidths free for voice transmission.

At @

This character is always present in any e-mail address: it is placed between the username and the domain name.

Attachment

A document that accompanies an e-mail message.

Banner ad

An advertisement placed on a Web site for a fee. Click the image to go to the advertiser's site.

Bookmark or **Favorite**

An electronic bookmark available in browsers that allows you to keep a note of the addresses of your favourite Web pages on your hard disk.

Bps (bits per second)

(1 bit per second = 1 baud, 1kps = 1000 bits per second, 1mps = 1000kps) The unit used to measure the speed of data transmission over the Internet, and the speed of a modem.

Browser

The software you need in order to be able to see Web pages. You cannot edit pages using this tool.

Byte

A string that is 8 bits long: each letter of the alphabet is described by a byte. Bytes are used to measure the size of files. 1 K (kilo-byte) = 1000 bytes; 1 M (mega-byte) = 1000 K; 1 G (giga-byte) = 1000 M.

Cache

A copy of the pages you visit is stored in a part of your hard drive called the cache. If you display the same page twice in a row, it will take less time to display the page the second time, because the page is loaded from your hard drive, not the Internet.

Chat

"Rooms" on the Internet in which you can have live, online conversations.

Client/server

A computer which is set up to provide a service to clients. For example, a Web site is hosted by a server, and your browser is the client who asks the server to display a page from the site on your computer.

Compression

The technique of transforming a file in order to reduce its size.

Connection

Connecting a computer to a network. Your computer needs to be connected to the Internet before you can access its services.

Cookie

A file sent to your computer by a Web site. Information in this file while be re-read by the site the next time you visit.

Cracker

A pirate programmer who breaks the "locks" in a software application in order to use it without paying, thus illegally.

Cryptology

The technology of encoding: encrypting texts or data so that only recipients who have the decoding key can read them.

DNS (Domain Name Server)

A computer that converts each domain name as we read them into the corresponding numeric IP address.

Domain - domain name

A name reserved on the Internet to designate a Web site. For example, www.eni-publishing.com is the domain name that belongs to ENI Publishing.

Download

Transferring files, or software, from the Internet to your computer.

E-mail

Private message sent over the Internet, from and to users with an e-mail address. They are no more private than a postcard is.

Electronic-mail

see E-mail.

Extension

The last letters in a file or domain name, separated by a full stop. For example: myfile.xls; www.eni-publishing.com

Extranet

A collection of Web pages, some of which are accessible to anyone via the Internet, others that are reserved for users of an intranet.

FAQ (Frequently Asked Questions)

In a forum, read the FAQ before you ask any questions. This is one of the basic rules of "netiquette".

File format

All computing files are encoded in 0 and 1, but an image file is not the same as a text file and cannot be read using the same software. Furthermore, there are several types of image file, and not all graphics programs can read all image file types. These different file types are called formats and, on a PC, can be recognised according to the last three letters at the end of the file name. These three letters are called the extension.

Firewall

A control technique that aims to allow access to a private network (such as an intranet) only to authorised users.

Freeware

Contraction of free software.

FTP (File Transfer Protocol)

The "language", or protocol, used to transport files over the Internet.

GIF (Graphic Interchange Format)

A file format with a limit of 256 available colours. It is very popular on the Internet.

Hacker

Pirate programmer who breaks through firewalls in order to access sites and private networks. Most do this for fun, some for gain.

Homepage

The first page to appear when you visit a site. A very important page, playing the role of both cover page and contents page.

HTML (HyperText Markup Language)

The language used to create Web pages and insert images into pages.

HTTP (HyperText Transfer Protocol)

The "language" or protocol used to transfer Web pages over the Internet.

Hypertext

A group of pages with no specific structure, linked together via hyperlinks and links. The Web is a hypertext that includes over a billion pages.

IMAP (Internet Message Access Protocol)

The protocol that allows you to access an e-mail mailbox on your ISP's computer. It is more powerful than POP3, and will eventually replace it.

Internet

Contraction of **Inter**connected **net**works: a network of all the networks that use the TCP/IP protocol.

Internet Explorer

Microsoft's Web browser. It was developed in record time in a bid to win back the huge share of the market that Netscape had conquered.

Internet Protocol or **IP**

The "language" or protocol used to transmit all the data that passes over the Internet. This data is divided into small packets, and different packets can travel over different routes. The packets are reconstructed at the destination by the TCP protocol.

Intranet

A private network that uses the same techniques as the Internet: TCP/IP protocols, FTP, e-mail, Web pages, and so on.

IRC (Internet Relay Chat)

Internet Chat using specific tools.

ISDN (Integrated Services Digital Network)

A digital, high throughput line used for dial-up access in place of a standard telephone line.

ISP (Internet Service Provider)

Company that offers an Internet connection service to private users.

JPEG (Join Picture Expert Group)

Image file format, which is particularly well-adapted for use with photographs and is used a lot on the Web. This format was created by a group of independent experts, which is where the name comes from.

Links

see Hypertext.

Mail

see E-mail

MIME (Multi-purpose Internet Mail Extension)

Compression standard that has been adapted for files attached to e-mail messages.

Modem

Contraction of **mo**dulator - **dem**odulator: a tool that can transmit the messages that computers send to each other over telephone lines. A telephone for computers.

MPEG (Motion Picture Expert Group)

Video file format created by a group of independent experts, hence the name.

MP3

Contraction of MPEG 2 layer 3: the audio part of an MPEG video file. As the compression quality is very high, this format is very popular for music files on the Internet.

Netiquette

Contraction of **N**etwork **etiquette**: defines the rules for Internet life.

Netscape Navigator

Netscape's Web browser, it was the first commercially viable browser.

Newsgroup

An Internet discussion forum that may or may not be public. The discussions are not real-time (not live). Synonyms include: forums, discussion groups, discussion forums, message boards.

Online - offline

Working online means that your computer is connected to the Internet, and offline is when you are not connected. When you retrieve your e-mail, you need to go online, but you can then disconnect and consult them offline.

Plug-in

A small, free program that completes a software. If your browser is not complete enough, you can add to it with plug-ins that will increase its performance, notably its multimedia functions.

POP

Post Office Protocol: the protocol that ensures your outgoing mail is sent. The current version is 3: POP3.
Point of Presence: the closest Internet access point to any given computer.

Portal

A site that offers a complete service that is of sufficient quality to generate a high number of loyal users. Any ambitious company would prefer to have a portal rather than a site.

Provider

see ISP

Proxy

This sort of server is installed by an ISP to keep a copy of the most popular Web pages, which means that the ISP's subscribers can access these pages more quickly.

Referencing

This is the act of giving the address of a site you have created to a search engine. The search engine will manually (if it is a directory) or automatically (if it is an index) visit the site and "reference" it.

Search engine

An automated library. Ask it what you are looking for, generally using keywords and it will suggest a list of pages that should correspond to your search.

Shareware

Software, often created by an independent programmer, that you can try for free, then pay its creator if you want to keep it.

Signature

Short text that is automatically added to the end of an e-mail. It generally contains the contact details of the sender, but may also include a quote, or thought for the day.

Site

A collection of Web pages that are produced by the same person or company, and have the same domain name.

Smiley

Symbols for indicating the tone of a message: **:-)** smiling, happy; **:-(** sad; **;-)** cheeky (a wink) and so on. They are used in e-mails, in forums, online chats, etc.

Spam - spamming

Spam is the name for unwanted mail you receive by e-mail, which may be publicity, or a free-prize draw entry, for example (the same sort of "junk" mail you might receive by the post). You should signal any spam to your ISP, who will take the necessary action.

TCP/IP

The two protocols used to transport data over the Internet.

Thread

The development of a discussion in a forum, as several users reply publicly to a message.

Trojan

An unwanted program which, once on your computer, allows a hacker to access the computer and its hard drives.

URL (Uniform Resource Locator)

Standardisation of Web addresses, which aims to make linking easier between separate sites.

Username

The name by which an Internet user is identified. In order to connect, you need your username and password.

Usenet

A network of computers that host forums.

Virus

A short, unwanted program that is destined to infect as many computers as possible. Viruses are often transmitted via e-mail, but are only activated if you open an infected attachment.

Webcam

A little camera used for sending images to a computer.

Webmaster

The administrator of a Web site. The editorial Webmaster is in charge of the site's content, whereas the technical Webmaster ensures that all the pages in the site are accessible to users.

Webpage

The building block of a Web site. Some Web pages contain hundreds of pages. A browser shows only one page at a time.

Website

see Site

Websurfer

Internet user who browses the Web - you!

World Wide Web

The hypertext "library" on the Internet. It contains over a billion Web pages (constructed using HTML), which are linked together by hyperlinks and which are called using the HTTP protocol in order to be displayed in a user's browser.

Worm

Short, unwanted program that can reproduce itself on a computer to such an extent as to use up all the machine's resources and render it useless.

Index

A

B

C

Index

Index

Index

Index

Index